OSCAR WILDE

OSCAR WILDE

Philosopher, Poet and Playwright

JAMES HODGSON

GREENWICH EXCHANGE
LONDON

Greenwich Exchange, London

First published in Great Britian in 2017
All rights reserved

Oscar Wilde: Philosopher, Poet and Playwright
© James Hodgson 2017

Printed and bound by www.imprintdigital.com
Typesetting and layout by Jude Keen Ltd, London
Tel: 020 8355 4541

Cover image ©Alamy Images
Cover design: December Publications 07951 511275

Greenwich Exchange Website: www.greenex.co.uk

Cataloguing in Publication Data is available
from the British Library.

ISBN: 978-1-910996-10-2

For my family and friends

ACKNOWLEDGEMENTS

I wish gratefully to acknowledge the support given by the late Martin Seymour-Smith, Anthony Fowles, Warren Hope, the late Robert Nye, Henry Maas, Peter Randall, Maggie Andrews, Roger Luxton and Andrew Keanie, all of whom have challenged and encouraged me to complete this book.

I wish to thank Janet Davidson, Patrick Ramsey and Jude Keen for the making of this book.

'O Ages! O Towers! Who is blameless?'

Rimbaud

CONTENTS

Preface

A WORD ABOUT THE GENESIS OF this book: it arose from those continual discussions about literature and philosophy I had with Martin Seymour-Smith (1928–98), the poet and critic, in what proved to be the last years of his life. His sharp and independent mind led him to the conclusion, expressed in his *Modern World Literature*, that Wilde had 'undue influence'. Seymour-Smith knew that I found interest in Wilde's work, so he said that I needed to challenge that interest. Typically he urged that I should explore *why* I thought what I did.

It has taken me an inordinately long time to do just that. This was partly due to the uncertainty I created for myself – Wilde's poetry was inadequate? His plays, except *The Importance of Being Earnest*, were merely society melodramas? And so on. It took some time to test and formulate what I really thought. There have been the exigencies of earning a living and the repetitive strain injury of the soul that ensues. Actually, the real reason was, as Dr Johnson (*Lives of the English Poets*) said of Alexander Pope's delay in producing his translation of *The Iliad*:

> ... According to this calculation the progress ... may seem to have been slow; but the distance is commonly great between actual performances and speculative possibility. It is natural to suppose that as much as has been done to-day may be done tomorrow; but on the morrow some difficulty emerges, or some external impediment obstructs. Indolence, interruption, business, and pleasure all take their turns in retardation ... He that runs against Time has an antagonist not subject to casualties.

Wilde's work and intellectual outlook have been overshadowed by his biography. He should be remembered instead for his work and in that work, his thought processes. By most accounts he was a delightful companion, who sought to, and did, amuse; his plays delight us still, as do what is recorded of his *bons mots*. Without detracting from that, this book attempts to answer why his work should be remembered, and to give a provisional answer at least to his lasting achievements. His work flowed from an intellectual standpoint which evolved from his time at Trinity College, Dublin, through Oxford into his mature years. He tried to make sense of our existence, of our passions, especially the erotic, as well as of our knowledge of how society is and of how it might be. His standpoint was undoubtedly based upon his aesthetic sense, which is why he found the doctrines of art for art's sake appealing, as he did Walter Pater's clarion call to live for the moment. There is a central philosophical strand to his work which is rarely far from view. This book sees him as a philosopher, gives credit to him as a poet and assesses his drama. It is written, finally, from a sympathetic but critical point of view: there would be no point in doing otherwise.

1

Introduction

OSCAR WILDE'S DIVIDED NATURE LED HIM most obviously to be the quintessential, decadent Parisian *boulevardier*, a creature of contemporary culture, a follower if not a creator of fashion – a Dandy, a *flâneur*. He saw himself as possessing taste beyond that of mere fashion, and had a gift for publicity which makes the *boulevardier* in him very modern indeed. Wilde would ideally idle away his days in conversation with congenial companions, preferably those whose critique of life did not involve strictures, beyond the gossipy kind, of sexual tastes. In such company he would shine, but also be able to develop his ideas to the accompaniment of appreciative murmurs.

He wanted also – in a contradictory sort of way – to be taken seriously as a writer and as an intellectual. It was the nature of his life and work to embrace opposites whether in religion, art or sex. He would have liked to see himself at the centre of the salon and literary life of Paris. His perspective was genuinely cosmopolitan. Paris could lay claim to being the most significant centre of art and culture. This was the Paris of recently constructed boulevards – where one could watch people pass by in an endless flow, parading to excite the attention of people seated in cafés. He appears in the *Journals* of the Goncourt brothers on his first visit to Paris (1882) as one '*au sexe douteux* … ' In England he was considered ' … a damn compromising fellow to be with … ' There, in the difference of expression, lies all the cultural differences of two countries. Actually, as it was for many of the wealthier open-minded people of his time – Paris was for him, too, only a retreat – the drama of his life and work was played out in London.

Wilde was a traveller: he moved from Dublin to Oxford, Oxford to London, travelling to Greece, Paris, the United States and North Africa. And, he brought back with him to London something from each of the cultures he encountered. He had a role as an interpreter and transferor of culture. He first brought what was Irish in him: the genuine gift of conversation, a generosity of spirit and a love of learning. From Oxford he brought aestheticism and a reinforced obsession for things Greek (including what the later 19th century styled the 'Greek' love between men). His sojourn in America developed an amused view of the States and its commercial materialism. But above all, it is what he gleaned from French literary culture – the aesthetics of Gautier, Baudelaire, Verlaine, Mallarmé, Huysmans and a profound love and understanding of Balzac – that was remarkable for that time in England.

Wilde had a desire for fame, and a macabre taste for notoriety: 'The only thing worse than being talked about – is not being talked about.' And there in a moment, in that sentence, with its insight into human frailty – without pretending not to be part of it – it is possible to grasp why his memory survives. Wilde managed to stand above those thousands of *boulevardiers* whose lives have now all but disappeared into a kind of background blur of colour – suggesting the passing by of a person rather than its actuality, reminiscent of Charles Conder's paintings of the same epoch: see especially *Les Passants*. Wilde's story – told endlessly – continues to hold the attention of successive generations of readers. His private acceptance of his sexuality, his public mask adopted for the sake of certain proprieties and the avoidance of scandal, and finally his defiant courtroom appearance strike a note with anyone who has lived candidly with self-knowledge.

Fascinating though it may be, this is not the main concern of this book, which is to explore the claim to fame which he would rather have had – namely, the value of his literary work. Unlike Balzac whom he unreservedly admired, or Dickens whose work he castigated – 'One would have to have a heart of stone not to laugh at the death of Little Nell'

– to read Wilde one does not have to read an armful of books many of which are master works in themselves. He is rather like Dryden, of whom Dr Johnson said the evidence of his genius is there in ' … the atoms of probability … scattered all over his works'. But Wilde did not have Dryden's vast output: and where Dryden struggled as a dramatist, Wilde succeeded, and where Wilde may have fallen short as a poet, Dryden certainly triumphed. Both were accomplished essayists. Both were born as Protestants and died as Catholics, when these things mattered. There the resemblance ends – Dryden shifted English poetry into its Augustan mode: but Wilde did not have the same effect on drama or on poetry. He did achieve, long after his death, some recognition for the ambisexual way of life. The ' … love that dare not tell its name … ', the love between people of the same sex, is still love and, as with heterosexuality, lust also. And with humour, and detachment, but not hostility, he was able to review the marriage market of his day, in such a way as is still capable of resonance. He belongs to a select few of moralists capable of showing our faults and follies, but not pretending to be untouched by these failings: 'We are all in the gutter, but some of us are looking at the stars.' On the moral plane, of course, detractors will say that he did much (unintended) harm – to his wife, who loved him deeply, and to those young men whom he used, to his children, who suffered from his reputation all of their lives – but at the same time he is shown to have done much good

– he was generous with his affection, time and money to poets, friends and others whose paths he crossed. In the final balance of these things, who is to say?

For one who boasted of idleness, and who affected to disdain ' … the vulgar test of production … ' ('Pen, Pencil and Poison') he was remarkably industrious. And for one who wished to see his work as art, he produced relatively little, and of that only a fraction might enter the lists as living up to his own critical standards. Fear of failure, fear of discovery of his sexuality – in a time when British society persecuted male homosexuality (absurdly, given its incidence) – made him adopt poses or roles – 'masks' he preferred to say. All of the leading characters in his prose and plays have guilty secrets and flirt with disclosure. This sense of danger was a source of excitement for Wilde, and one of the spurs to his creativity.

In looking at his work, as with every writer, the privileges of personality must be set aside in the quest for what is enduring rather than that which is mainly historical. The common ground is the work, as it might be judged by one whom Dr Johnson entitled, so aptly, the common reader. Wilde affected to despise the work, saying that he had put only his talent into his work but his genius into his life. 'In Pen, Pencil and Poison', he referred to the poisoner Wainewright as a Dandy, said by Charles Lamb to be the writer of 'capital prose', who was not to be judged in commonplace terms. This was Wilde, writing as ever he did, about – himself. He would write capital prose, and rightly not be judged by the vulgar test of production – if that means quantity, but by his achievement. Far from disdaining what people thought about his work he vigorously contested, through his letters to newspapers and journals, any critical voice that did not concur with his own. He fought for a place in English letters, accumulating fame, seeking to dominate and lead – which for a time he did. He would have liked to do the same in France too. Viewed conventionally, his progress was interrupted by his trials and public humiliation – a very Victorian dénouement to what was a Victorian life. That is all history: not without interest, but not what we are looking for.

2

Influences on Wilde

WHO WAS WILDE, THE WRITER? THIS question of identity on the levels of personality and work puzzled his contemporaries and eludes many of his biographers, the latter so often wanting to label him in order to judge both him and his work. He said of himself that he stood 'in symbolic relations to the art and culture of my age' – and he thought if someone could not remain wholly ignorant, 'a pure bloom', the only resort was to be 'over-educated'. He was the latter. His relationship to his age is demonstrated in *The Picture of Dorian Gray*, where Gray (one of his *alter egos*) explores, Faust-like, ancient and modern literature, whilst his *Oxford Notebooks* show his keen interest in ancient (classical Greek) and contemporary philosophy. The *Notebooks* show that he was concerned to understand, challenge and move philosophical thought forward. Further, he wanted to *live* his philosophical findings. Bravado made him declare his genius, before it had borne fruit. As a result many of his contemporaries were too apt to write him off as a *poseur*, lacking any depth of thought. Other more perceptive people sensed a significant movement of mind in a learned and thoughtful man. He was indeed very well read and well educated: a classicist, fluent in ancient and modern languages, winning scholarships – albeit denied (because of his espousal of Aestheticism) a university career. He was also a keen observer and avid learner, apt to absorb influences rapidly but not always to his advantage, and prone to *mimesis* as the way in which to be *creative*. Was his contribution more than the sum of its parts? He synthesised different strands of thought – but why did he? There was a 'project' or purpose. It was immensely ambitious. He was seeking to understand the world, as well as his own nature and place in it. He sought to universalise his findings: he wanted to correct the misapprehensions of his and to an extent of any age too – to change the way we live. This was true whether in the realm of 'beauty' and art, in society with its extremes of poverty and wealth, or in the expression of love and sexuality. It was a broad front he was attempting to move along: it was not simply, as is so often supposed, the narrower one of homosexual orientation. The question of sexual orientation, though, was one that stimulated him and motivated him to provide answers that stood up to rigorous examination. His was the 'examined life' and that interrogation was conducted through his work.

* * *

Oscar Wilde was born on 16th October 1854, of parents who belonged to Ireland's intellectual elite. They were at the centre of Dublin's social and intellectual life. His parents were both Irish nationalists. Ireland was in an increasingly disputed union with Great Britain that ended mostly in the early 20th century. His mother, Lady Wilde, whom he adored and whose good opinion he always wanted, was a nationalist poet whose pen name was Speranza. Her fame amongst Irish nationalists guaranteed him the warmest of receptions in the United States when he toured there giving lectures, in the 1880s.

Although nominally Protestant, Speranza had Oscar baptised into the Roman Catholic faith to indicate his Irish identity. The religious question (no less than the question of identity) was to follow Wilde throughout his life – he thought on at least two occasions of becoming a Catholic before his deathbed conversion in 1900. This lack of resolution, moving towards yet away, is the man. He could be described also as Freemason, pagan or agnostic – but the old religion never entirely went away.

Wilde himself was always a Home Ruler, and despite his carefully elocuted English accent, his love of Oxford and life in London, his sense of Irish identity remained. Had he stayed in Ireland he would have been, almost certainly, active in the Irish Nationalist movement. He was in any event a warm supporter of Parnell, and generously supported Nationalists as well as other radicals even when it did his reputation harm. Apart from nationalistic considerations, one theme stands out with Wilde: he understood, as do all Irish people, the nature of oppression. Ireland had a ruling class, mostly of alien origin, that owned the land – the only means of production – and extorted rents, and often chose to live anywhere but Ireland. This knowledge of imperialism and its wrongdoing was stark and unavoidable. An Englishman, as Dr Johnson remarked, believes he is free even though he is in prison; this type of illusion is not found usually amongst Irish people. This intrinsic grasp of alienation made Wilde sympathetic to the claims of both socialism and anarchism. These claims he followed through by supporting artists, poets and others who fell foul of the Establishment. No amount of Dublin snobbery (as Shaw saw it) or class consciousness (Wilde was apt to stand on his dignity as a 'gentleman' when he was losing an argument) obliterated this humane impulse. And behind it stands the shade of Speranza.

His father, Sir William Wilde, was an eminent eye surgeon, and moreover an archaeologist, author and antiquarian. He might have been a father wholly to admire – except for his public sexual adventures with women, upon whom he fathered a number of children, and a sex scandal and trial that erupted when Oscar was at school. Wilde never forgave his father for this public humiliation of his mother, and when Sir William lay dying, his love for his mother was never greater than when she allowed Sir William's mistress to sit at his bedside. 'All women become like their mothers. That is their tragedy. No man does. That is his', as a woman character says in one of his plays. Wilde's thraldom to his mother was to have a last, fatal consequence: she was determined that Oscar should go through the trial that ruined him – she was persuaded of his innocence – he was better than his father after all, but just to make it clear, she would never speak to him if he ran away (the most 'sensible' course of action urged upon him by anxious friends). Constance Wilde did not detach the son from the formidable mother, rather seeing in her the love that her own early life lacked. Nor would Oscar's love for young men seriously detract from Speranza's influence. Sir William's learning and scholarship was Oscar's inheritance – and that was considerable. Sexual adventures, scholarly pursuits, poetry, religion, politics and gossip all contribute to the ease with which later Wilde was able to write his plays that reflect on the gap between the real and the ideal.

The children of the Wilde household were not sent to bed before evening dinner but were allowed to hear adults speak, argue and gossip at the dining table and, when old enough, say ten years old, as the French then did, to drink wine. In later life the dinner table is where he sought to shine and dominate with charm and fluent talk testing out his ideas. It is in part the explanation of his love of dialogue in his written work.

Oscar was the younger of the two Wilde sons. His elder brother, William, was relatively untalented, later becoming a journalist and, dogged by a sense of personal failure, an alcoholic. There was a younger sister, Isola the girl much wanted by Speranza: tragically, she died in infancy. The grief this must have given Speranza can only be guessed – and the loss is commemorated by Oscar in the brief, beautiful poem 'Requiescat'.

The Wilde family had, in short, a good social position – a fact vital to life and livelihoods in the Victorian world. This position had to be upheld by ostensible conduct – 'respectability' and income or wealth (capital), preferably both. It was a world that was largely dominated by males, whose role was to provide the key ingredients of successful family life – to be in an eminent or recognised position, and to provide the money via a profession or acquire it through marriage or inheritance. Sir William achieved genuine eminence, the appearance of wealth and income, and the façade of respectability. The latter collapsed in a sexual scandal and public trial, and the former on Sir William Wilde's death in 1876 when he left the family with considerably less wealth than they expected, or that their social position in Dublin life required. The contrast between the 'image' of social position and its reality is a key theme of Wilde's writings, especially his later comedies of manners. The reconciliation of these conflicts is via love. It is no wonder that the Argentinian writer Borges saw in Wilde's work not tragedy but optimism and hope.

Trinity College

Wilde went first to Trinity College, Dublin. At this time, Trinity was the preserve of the largely Unionist Protestant and Anglo-Irish Ascendancy. Wilde would not have been seen to be out of place, although his nationalism was a point of difference. Examinations at Trinity were oral rather than written, the ability persuasively to express what one knew was of paramount importance. This talent was not only Wilde's calling card, but the key to his creative processes. Extemporising in front of an audience gave him the fluidity to test out ideas and learn from the reaction to what he was saying. Deprived of an audience, how was he to create? He was to find just this difficulty in his years of exile at the end of his life.

Wilde's tutor at Trinity was Pentland Mahaffy – a noted classicist, and, later, author of *The Art of Conversation*. Wilde was rather patronisingly to review this work as 'jejune'. The difference between the two men was in all probability, political – Mahaffy was a Unionist. Mahaffy took Wilde with him to Greece to see the Parthenon and other sights. This was no mean enterprise. Greece was then infested with brigands and it was not a journey lightly to be undertaken. The hoped-for visit to Rome *en route*, with its classical and Catholic connotations, was not affordable. Mahaffy's love of things Greek – and the openness of the Greek classics on same-sex love – both left their welcome impression on Oscar. Wilde gained a scholarship to Oxford University, which changed his perspective on his life permanently.

Oxford

Wilde, if not thoroughly Irish, could be described as truly Oxonian. He loved Oxford and the companions he found there. The ideal of attractive young men with the leisure to study and when not, to idle, was exemplified, and when past, anxiously sought again. So avid was he for Oxford's acceptance he took elocution lessons to remove or transmute his Dublin accent. His carefully modulated tones thereafter were to be used to beguile friends and foes alike. He was able to extend his life as a student until his mid-twenties. His work shows that had he not opted for the open and controversial espousal of aestheticism; in all probability he would have been accepted as a scholar of the classics. Whilst at Oxford his mind was opened to the higher end of intellectual life. The more obvious influences will be commented upon shortly, but what is clear both from the internal evidence of his work as well as the *Notebooks* is that he absorbed the influence of not only

Greek classical authors but also of Greek philosophy: especially Plato. In the simile of the Cave in *The Republic*, mankind is likened to a prisoner who is chained up in such a way as to see only the shadows of things cast by torches in the cave, and not the real things themselves. It means that we are in our ordinary lives at best hazarding at the truth. The doctrine of Heraclitus that all is in flux means that what is seen to be true now is not the moment before or after: 'You never step into the same river twice.' Plato's search for what is unchangingly true led him to the theory of forms, sometimes misdescribed as the 'ideal'. Wilde understood all of this – but additionally sought to integrate the modern with this set of ideas. Hegel with his model of dialectical reasoning – thesis, antithesis and then synthesis – seemed to Wilde to be a way of approaching the truth: 'The truth is rarely pure, and never simple.'

Arnold, Ruskin, Pater and J.A. Symonds

Matthew Arnold had an enormous influence on Victorian thought. This operated on a number of levels. In poetry, he captured the imagination of the age through a handful of poems: 'Thyrsis', 'The Scholar Gipsy', 'Balder Dead' and 'Dover Beach'. Above all, 'Dover Beach' sums up the crisis of faith amongst intellectuals – whether it was discovery of the antiquity of the earth – which meant that science showed that the world was a lot older than implied by the Bible (and if this was true, what was the truth of the entire book?) or the impact of Darwin's *On the Origin of Species* which compounded the doubt about the biblical account of the creation of Man.

> The sea of faith
> Was once, too, at the full, and round earth's shore
> Lay like the folds of a bright girdle furl'd.
> But now I only hear
> Its melancholy, long, withdrawing roar ...
>
>   (from 'Dover Beach')

Wilde, amongst many others needed to respond to this – which he endeavoured to do in the first place, through his poetry, as well as his philosophic musings in his commonplace books. This purpose underpins much of Wilde's work. Arnold advocated seriousness evidenced by the manner of composition. Wilde was actually serious but advocated quite the opposite in manner. Arnold's attitudes are still perpetuated, and as a result Wilde's work and that of other wits has suffered. Arnold's *Culture and Anarchy* forms part of the backdrop to Wilde's essays. Arnold's 'Requiescat ' was also the model of Wilde's poem with the same title:

> *Arnold*:
> Strew on her roses, roses,
> And a never a spray of yew!
> In quiet she reposes;
> Ah, would that I did too!

Wilde:
Tread lightly, she is near
Under the snow,
Speak gently, she can hear
The daisies grow ...

... I vex my heart alone,
She is at rest ...

... All my life's buried here,
Heap earth upon it.

Of the two poems, it must be said that Oscar's has it.

Wilde's possible progress as a professional scholar at Oxford was intellectually halted by two men. The first was John Ruskin. Ruskin tried, at the level of reason, to save British taste whether in products, buildings or art from its unerring love of the mediocre. He looked at architecture, in his *The Stones of Venice* or his *The Bible of Amiens*, to discover the meaning and importance of these art forms. In painting he championed especially Turner at a time when Turner was regarded as merely eccentric or the 'over Turner' of art, and ensured the survival of many of his major works. Ruskin was a kind of socialist, ashamed of the social and aesthetic conditions of his time. Symbolically, he spent his own money to ensure that the approaches to the British Museum were swept clean. His lectures persuaded Wilde that aesthetics was a matter of conscience and went hand in hand with good works. At Ruskin's suggestion,

Wilde and other students built a road to help some villagers in Oxfordshire. Socialism of a kind, but not hard physical labour, stayed with Wilde, as did, more significantly, proselytising about the role of beauty and art.

Walter Pater (1839–94) had still greater influence on Wilde. His dogmas about art and its function in life were subjective and sensual contrasted with Ruskin's public and moralistic conceptions. Pater's ideas, based somewhat loosely on post-Kantian German philosophy, were doubly attractive to Wilde. Here was a justification for living a hedonistic life: it was moral because it was what life was:

> ... not the fruit of experience, but experience itself, is the end ... How shall we pass most swiftly from point to point, and be present always at the focus where the greatest number of vital forces unite in their purest energy? To burn always with this hard, gemlike, flame ... is success in life ... not to discriminate every moment some passionate attitude in those about us, and in the very brilliancy of their gifts some tragic dividing of forces on their ways, is, on this short day of frost and sun, to sleep before evening.
> (*The Renaissance*, 1873 edition)

And yet it was free from convention. Pater was able to write about the situation of same-sex passion in his essay on Winckelmann – especially Winckelmann's death at the hands of a petty thief. What Pater wrote about, Wilde endeavoured to live. That was the difference of temperament between the two men. Pater again:

... For art comes to you proposing frankly to give nothing
but the highest quality to your moments as they pass, and
simply for those moments' sake. (ibid.)

Wilde never lost his respect for Pater. Pater later loyally (but
not uncritically) reviewed *The Picture of Dorian Gray* on its
appearance in book form.

In certain respects John Addington Symonds (1840–93),
an Oxford man but he had left Oxford by the time Wilde
arrived there, is no less significant in Wilde's development.
He was a critic, historian and poet, a man of conflicted
sexual desires – married but also passionately homosexual.
He was as strong an advocate of recognition of same-sex
relationships and desires as the age permitted. He saw merit
in them: the model was Greek – the love of an older man for
a younger, the protégé – but also potentially more than that.
In 1883 he published *A Problem in Greek Ethics* which he
had written 10 years earlier, which deals as openly as may be
with such relationships. Wilde reviewed Symonds' work,
and in the *Oxford Notebooks*, he cites Symonds' biography
of Shelley. Symonds saw merit in Wilde's poetry, and
sympathetically reviewed 'The Portrait of Mr W.H.' But
although appreciative of *The Picture of Dorian Gray*, which
he thought ' ... artistically and psychologically interesting',
he thought it also to be ' ... unwholesome in tone ... '

Whistler

After Wilde became a leading aesthete at Oxford he made a friend of James Whistler, the painter who led the Art for Art's sake movement. But Whistler, a man of sharp wit and an innate sense of his own eminence, did not see Wilde so much as a friend as a disciple. This was Whistler's way: he shamefully used the time of the Greaves brothers (instead of encouraging their artistic endeavours) to row him about the Thames the better to obtain the views he needed. The essence of friendship is a kind of equality – of affection, respect, understanding which is reciprocated. Wilde, not being content for long with a subordinate role, began to express his own opinions. Their relationship became competitive. Whistler was enraged by Wilde's increasing influence, and Wilde did not like the lack of respect he got from Jimmy Whistler. Their friendship broke up noisily, and destructively. This competitiveness and destructiveness surfaced later in Wilde's relations with Bosie (Lord Alfred Douglas). Whistler's influence did productively endure: in *Intentions* it is asserted that Nature imitates Art, that London did not have fogs until Whistler painted them. What does this mean? It is wilfully close to absurdity. The Wildean paradox, essentially an inversion often done for comic effect, challenges banal conceptions of truth and rationality: the flaw, if there is one, is that more is needed than a *bon mot* – the appetite is whetted, but its satisfaction is less easily obtained.

America and the Lectures on Art

After University, with little money and no real prospects, Wilde failed to obtain a post of Inspector of Schools. He found that trying to make a living from poetry or journalism and being a society figure did not yet pay the bills, especially his: he made an art form of extravagance. Being renowned in Britain as a leading figure of the Aesthetic Movement, he was invited to go on a lecture tour of the United States to publicise the Movement, which Gilbert and Sullivan's operetta *Patience* satirised, to ensure that operetta's success. It was a gamble for both Wilde and the promoters of *Patience*, and is an example of self-validating public relations campaigns. Wilde seized the opportunity and made it his own. He wrote lectures which set out his credo. Driven by the need to satisfy a public demand and to earn money, he set about making a *succès de scandale*, from the moment he arrived saying, 'I have nothing to declare but my genius' to amused Customs men and the press. He showed, throughout his working life a strong business sense. The tour was a success – helped by organising committees of expatriate Irish people determined to support Speranza's son. Whilst in the States he visited, significantly, Walt Whitman, whose poetry eulogised male 'friendships' and who felt compelled to deny his sexuality even to Symonds. Wilde also met and learned from the Irish playwright Dion Boucicault (1820–90) – who knew more about writing popular plays than anyone

– he wrote *The Colleen Bawn* which was a constant favourite amongst playgoers in Ireland and the States in the 19th century. Wilde saw the possibility of commercial success in the theatre. He wrote his play *Vera* and hoped to underpin potential success by recruiting Mary Anderson, the popular American actress, to play the lead role. *Vera* was 'prentice work, and success in the theatre had to wait.

Paris and then London

Wilde went to Paris after his American tour. He wanted to repeat his success there: he certainly succeeded in being noticed – the Goncourt Journals noted his ambiguous sexuality. And he was able to hold his own in conversation. He set about meeting French poets and intellectuals. He immersed himself in French culture: he read all of Balzac in his stay in Paris. He saw in Baudelaire, Verlaine, Mallarmé and others the possibilities of a change of style in his poetry. He could see potential to move forward his own views on art and life. He returned to London with still no prospects but with a new style – no longer sporting his costume as an Aesthete but as a Dandy. (The meaning of Dandy is explored later in the chapter on *Dorian Gray*.) Journalism and lecturing seemed the obvious resort to make money. There are shades of Maupassant's *Bel Ami* in his methods.

Constance Wilde

Speranza urged marriage on her sons – it would help solve the problem of being impecunious and thus unable to hold the Wildes' station in life. This was the convention of the time. Some believe it provided Oscar with the cover he needed to carry on his same-sex life. There really is no evidence to support this contention: he was curious about same-sex relations, *croyant* perhaps but not yet *pratiquant*. Where the evidence does point is that Wilde did love women – more than 'liking' them. He was in love with Florence Balcombe, who later married Bram Stoker, the author of *Dracula*, and was downcast when she rejected him. He loved, or thought he did, Lillie Langtry. But unquestionably, he loved Constance Lloyd whom he married in 1884. The grilling he got from Constance's grandfather about his economic prospects surfaced later in his plays: Lady Bracknell in *The Importance of Being Earnest* quizzing Jack Worthing about his wealth and prospects.

Wilde settled in London with his young bride, and Speranza came too – but she received a Civil List pension to help live in what was considered to be an appropriate way for a person of her station. He went every week to her salon; and her influence over him never truly waned.

Wilde, in common with many men of his time, used prostitutes – it was considered privately, in a smoking-room kind of way ('respectable' women did not smoke) to be acceptable ('sowing wild oats') until marriage. His letters show that he slept with a famous Parisian prostitute when he lived there in the early 1880s. He found it a necessary but not wholly attractive release. Something of this can be discerned in his poem, 'The Harlot's House'. He embarked upon marriage with great sexual enthusiasm – his attempts to describe his lovemaking to the young R.H. Sherard were too explicit for the younger, more idealistic man to endure. Wilde's notions of love did not preclude liaisons with other people – in this he was like his father, whether they were women (he still visited brothels), or more significantly, young men. He did not set out to be like his father, but it came about. The received wisdom is that Wilde should never have married, and that his relations with Constance were a 'cover' for his real life. But this is to confuse the end point of his sexual journey with the actual journey he took.

Constance, whilst admiring Wilde, was a thoughtful critic of his work. He showed her *Vera* – and she found some fault with it: and well she might: its shortcomings and unevenness are evident. She also became a writer. She was evidently a woman of considerable gifts, a noted society figure as well as a strong advocate of feminism and socialism. In their early days together they learned German. Oscar dressed her according to his view of modern dress for women. She gave him two sons – Cyril born in 1885, and Vyvyan in 1886. Her focus naturally enough became her family – and Oscar found himself with time on his hands when he was not treading the lecture circuit to get money to meet his new responsibilities. They drifted apart, in the conventional sense, quite quickly: but she was ever there, caring for his beloved sons, and providing a framework for Oscar's life that was to be led, increasingly, according to his passions. Even when it might be supposed that she was least influential, she can be discovered producing a book of his sayings *Oscariana* with the bookseller Humphreys with whom she had a brief liaison, and from whom the title of the play *An Ideal Husband* came.

Friends, Poets and Others

Wilde made friends, especially male friends, easily. His sexual longings were not always far from the surface: in the first years of his marriage he was writing to the student Harry Marillier asking for his photograph – and wondering when he might see him. And it was through his friendship with Robert Ross, who lodged in the Wilde household, that he discovered his joy in same-sex relations. He was later to affirm that it was 'little Robbie' who had seduced him. Wilde was 32 years old. This fact is also referred to in *The Picture of Dorian Gray*. He then embarked on 'that course of action', as one of his first biographers so quaintly puts it, that was to lead him to prison.

Victorian law made same-sex activity between males a crime: the same law did not apply to women – it was said, somewhat evasively, that Queen Victoria did not believe it existed. Today, it seems extraordinary that such a law should be enacted. Most people would think little of same-sex relations, provided, as with other sexual relations, there is no harm done nor is there coercion. Ross, according to his own testimony, wrote down much of what Wilde said and this was later used by Wilde in *The Picture of Dorian Gray* and in *Lady Windermere's Fan*. Wilde acknowledged Ross' role in the preparation of 'The Portrait of Mr W.H.', which is about Shakespeare's infatuation with a young man.

Wilde continued for a while to be heterosexually active – one brothel he visited he claimed taught him all he knew about sex. He abandoned Constance sexually, and sex with women, by about 1888. His life took on a duality: conventional marriage and family on the one hand and the pursuit of same-sex desire on the other. When he became commercially successful, he seemed to grow careless of this precarious balance: in his heart he must have known the risks he ran. Same-sex relations were forbidden by law. But whatever else, it was the occasion of an upsurge of excitement and creativity. Most of Wilde's output is concentrated in the years 1887–95.

He loved spending his time with young writers and especially poets – the object of friendship was not necessarily the prospect of a sexual liaison, but the pleasure of friendship itself, with its community of interest. Besides which, he needed an audience to enrapture, and in a gentle kind of way to dominate. It was how he developed his thoughts, expanded his repertoire of ideas and tested the audience's or reader's reaction. On such occasions he was not above purloining the wit of others. He once chided the young Max Beerbohm for his unusual reticence. Max replied that he feared that his wit 'might not prove faithful to me'. Wilde thought that 'The gods have bestowed on Max the gift of perpetual old age.' Max was not a poet but a talented essayist, caricaturist and Dandy. Max resented his own discipleship of Wilde, and repaid Wilde's sponsorship by collaborating spitefully with Robert Hichens in *The Green Carnation*, which satirised Wilde, Bosie and their circle and contributed to the general odium with which Wilde came to be regarded. Wilde riposted in *The Importance of Being Earnest*: 'Magley, Maxbohm … what ghastly names … '

Wilde was close to and lent support to a wide circle of poets: he loved this milieu the most. Key figures in England were: Richard Le Gallienne (1866–1947); John Gray (1866–1934), lover and friend – whose poetry he sponsored; W.B. Yeats (1865–1939); Ernest Dowson (1867–1900); Theodore Wratislaw (1871–1933); Victor Plarr (1863–1929) and Lionel Johnson (1867–1902). Whilst Yeats and Dowson are well known, Wratislaw's poetry repays reading. Johnson deserves more than a mention: he became a substantial critic, being the first to recognise Thomas Hardy's prose as art. The best of his poetry is unjustly neglected:

The Dark Angel

Dark Angel, with thine aching lust
To rid the world of penitence:
Malicious Angel, who still dost
My soul such subtile violence!

Because of thee, no thought, no thing,
Abides for me undesecrate:
Dark Angel, ever on the wing,
Who never reachest me too late! …

… Apples of ashes, golden bright;
Waters of bitterness, how sweet!
O banquet of a foul delight,
Prepared by thee, foul Paraclete! …

Which conveys the sense of temptation and sin (Apples of Ashes are the Apples of Sodom referred to by Milton in *Paradise Lost*). Johnson was also the cousin/friend of Lord Alfred Douglas (Bosie) (1870–1945) and had introduced him to Wilde. The loss of Bosie to Wilde he commemorated in 'The Destroyer of a Soul':

I hate you with a necessary hate …
… Mourning for that live soul, I used to see;
Soul of a saint, whose friend I used to be:
Till you came by! A cold, corrupting, fate …

Poems (1895)

Wilde stood bail for John Barlas (Evelyn Douglas) (1860–1914) – the anarchist poet who had fired a revolver at the Speaker's house in 1892, and if this were not sufficient, his poetry should be remembered:

A Rose in Water

A cut rose set in water, poor sick wraith,
Survives a little while in hectic bloom,
A ghostly body in a living tomb:
E'en as a love-sick maid it lingereth
Feeding its passion with protracted death;
While through the very wound that wrought its doom
It draws unnatural nourishment: the room
Is long time fragrant with its dying breath.
How slow life droops away cut off from thee,
But cannot wither, though inch by inch it dies!
Torn cruelly from love's mutilated tree,
Through my heart's wound I drink what grief supplies
Of waterish sustenance, salt as the sea;
And all the night is heavy with my sighs.

Love Sonnets 1889

The Significance of France

Wilde continued his admiration of French writers and French culture, which he duly absorbed, and used. This admiration – or rather affinity, remained with him throughout his life. As mentioned, during his stay in Paris in the early 1880s he took an apartment there, and even donned the monkish garb of Balzac to read *La Comédie*

Humaine in its entirety. He was to make use of the fictions of which he was in thrall:

> ' … one of the great tragedies of my life is the death of Lucien de Rubempré. It is a grief from which I have never been able completely to rid myself. It haunts me in my moments of pleasure … ' ('Decay of Lying')

He read Ernest Renan's *La Vie de Jésus* (Life of Jesus), which demystifies Christ and reinstates him as a human figure (the Son of Man). This work had a pervasive influence on Wilde's thought and methods. He used the parable, which is how Jesus' thought is represented to us through the New Testament: there is no doubt that Christ changed the way we think. Wilde in his turn really wanted to change the way we think – he chose to confront the conventional interpretation of religion, and to change it. He too, used parables together with a controversial analysis of what Jesus said – interpreted through Renan. Flaubert's *Trois Contes* and *La Tentation de Saint Antoine* inspired him further to use the religious mentality and sources as material. This can be seen in *Salomé, La Sainte Courtisane* as well as projects he discussed with André Gide which did not reach the light of day. Where his stories are recorded – for example 'The Early Church' (see Richard Ellmann's biography) he uses a story to entertain and make a philosophical point. His prose poems (emulating Baudelaire) refer directly or indirectly to religious/philosophical themes as in 'The Doer of Good',

'The Disciple' and 'The Master', and challenge the conventional view. He uses the Christ figure as the figure of compassion and suffering in his poems, including especially *The Ballad of Reading Gaol*, and in his prison letter to Lord Alfred Douglas, *De Profundis*.

Whilst in Paris he took steps to enter the French literary world: French culture was then at its height – and he met with some resistance (it was not until the 1890s that he managed to gain some form of acceptance). He met the Goncourt brothers who were rather dismissive of him, got to be friendly with Mallarmé (1842–98)and met Verlaine (1844–96). He was influenced, as was practically everyone of note on the French literary scene, by Baudelaire's work, Théophile Gautier, whose preface to *Mademoiselle de Maupin* spelt out the doctrine of Art for Art's sake, as well as by Verlaine's poetry, and perhaps above all by J.K. Huysmans' *À Rebours* (translated as 'Against the Grain' or 'Against Nature'). This served as one of the models for his *Dorian Gray*. It is different from *Gray*, and is vast in its analysis of the decadent spirit. It explores all the senses, conveying their exquisite pleasures until the appetite palls. This desolation left one critic wondering what the choices for Man are – religion or despair? Wilde's penultimate long poem, *The Sphinx*, rehearses this theme. In the 1890s he helped Verlaine to visit England. When he became a literary lion, he met André Gide (1869–1951) (whom he later took to a male brothel in Algeria). He was friends with Pierre

Louÿs (1870–1925) – whom he admired and who helped him with *Salomé*. Louÿs had a brief but productive writing career throughout the 1890s. His works, candid and erotic, remain in print. Subsequently Louÿs rejected Wilde because of Wilde's calculated indifference to Constance, but more significantly because of his friendship with Alfred Douglas: according to Wilde in his letter to More Adey in 1896: ' … Three years ago he asked me to choose between his friendship and my fatal connection with A.D. I need hardly say I chose at once the meaner spirit and a baser mind.'

Wilde borrowed from French writers, as did many of the 1890s 'decadent' school in Britain and Ireland.

Bosie

'Bosie' (Lord Alfred Douglas, 1870–1945) had literary interests as well as talent, but actually lacked the application that could have led to significant work, for which Wilde had hoped. Bosie's expensive lifestyle had the consequence that Wilde needed money incessantly, which drove him to write more plays under greater pressure. The effect was to produce two exceptional plays: *An Ideal Husband* and *The Importance of Being Earnest*. It steered Wilde away from the pitfalls of such productions as *Salomé*. The Wilde–Douglas relationship quickly became sexually competitive and both led each other on – hiring rent boys and leading a ruinously indiscreet sex life. Bosie's hostile relations with his father, the Marquess of Queensberry, caused him to draw Wilde into what was a family dispute: Wilde foolishly prosecuted Queensberry, who was out to humiliate his own son. In three trials Wilde's sex life came out in court – and, as befits the hypocrisy of Victorian England, his career as dramatist was ended, his social standing and family were destroyed. After two years of hard labour in prison (mainly in Reading) Wilde left England in 1897, never to return. His relationship with Bosie continued fitfully. Wilde died in Paris in 1900. Bosie commemorated Wilde, with some lines which show candid, deep feeling:

> **The Dead Poet**
> I dreamed of him last night, I saw his face
> All radiant and unshadowed of distress,
> And as of old, in music measureless,
> I heard his golden voice and marked him trace
> Under the common thing the hidden grace …
>
> *Sonnets (1909)*

No Audience – No Work

Wilde's motivation and method depended on two things – the ability to delight and test out ideas through conversation, and the ability to win over audiences, whether readers or theatre-going public. Both seemed, from his standpoint, to require social standing. Wilde assiduously cultivated his standing – he had known how to be controversial, entertaining, provocative even – but not to court rejection. His fall from public grace deprived him of all the audiences he knew how to work with. He produced no new plays (just the promise of them), but did write *The Ballad of Reading Gaol* which stands out in his poetry, and some letters to newspapers, but nothing further.

He was no Verlaine – much as he loved poetry he loved the comforts of life – and had no real desire to live a bohemian life. He also knew that his poetry was not of that standard either. Visiting Bohemia was quite all right; being in it all the time was not. He loved to dress for dinner, and to be in company. Constantly to be shunned in public was not just humiliating and hurtful; it deprived him of the point of going on. The loyalty of friends, whilst essential, does not make up entirely for the thrill of being in the world and encountering the new – and testing oneself against it. At the point where his writing might have delivered the promise that is there in those atoms of wit – it reached a blank wall. Witty as ever, perhaps a shade more reflective, deprived of his family, and with it the love he really needed and the attention he craved, his career and then his life painfully ended.

The drama of Wilde's rise to fame and then abrupt and disastrous fall has caught the attention of large numbers of biographers. Unsurprisingly, when writing about a life, the intimacies – especially those of sexual relations – become the focus. Much has been made of Wilde's sexuality, but it is his work and thought that make him interesting.

3

Poetry

POETRY WAS WILDE'S FIRST LOVE, AND he desired to be a poet. In his quest to be famous he wanted it to be for some substantial achievement. Perhaps, like Keats, he would be remembered. He started rather more conspicuously than did Keats. He won the Newdigate Prize at Oxford for his poem 'Ravenna' in 1878. His first book, *Poems* (1881), actually sold (unlike Keats') – helped by Wilde's gifts for self-publicity as he championed the Art for Art's sake movement. *Poems* was influenced by Pater's dictum that poetry 'aspires to the condition of music': it was divided into 'Movements', which was intended as a guide as to how it might be read. This was ambitious both in terms of aim but also in delivery: it asks a lot of a reader to see a theme in what is essentially individual and disparate.

Criticism was swift to follow. He was invited to place his book with the Oxford Union but such was the resentment of his celebrity that the offer was withdrawn, the official criticism being that it was really little more than a set of echoes of other men's work and there was no trace of him in it. This was a very serious charge. It was close enough to the reality, whilst misunderstanding what that reality was.

The charge of plagiarism or, more accurately, imitation was never to leave evaluations of Wilde's work, whether with regard to his poetry or in other fields of his literary endeavours. He was candid about his methods of work, as Robert Ross' introduction to *Salomé* (1912) plainly shows:

> Wilde complained to me one day that someone in a well-known novel had stolen an idea of his. I pleaded in defence of the culprit that Wilde himself was a fearless literary thief. 'My dear Robbie,' he said, with his usual drawling emphasis, 'when I see a monstrous tulip with four wonderful petals in someone else's garden, I am impelled to grow a monstrous tulip with five wonderful petals, but that is no reason why someone should grow a tulip with only three petals.' That was Oscar Wilde.

This really says it all. It is the key to how Wilde started his compositions. Monstrous tulips or not, his point of departure was the model given in the work of others. It is a common enough method used by literary people, along with unacknowledged translations (eg Baudelaire and *La*

Fanfarlo), but it does not necessarily follow that it is the sum total of what the work is. This facility of composition – handy enough to dash off copy quickly – leads also to difficulties.

Wilde did not, as did Coleridge, deal with the issues of plagiarism or imitation. In the Preface to *Christabel*, Coleridge gives the dates of composition of the two parts of the poem:

> The dates are mentioned for the exclusive purpose of precluding charges of plagiarism or servile imitation from myself ...

Coleridge's work is a significant influence on Wilde, both on the subject matter of the longer philosophical poems – 'Humanitad', 'Panthea' – as well as the manner of composition. Like many poets, Wilde was in a hurry to be a poet, that is, before he became one. In fairness, there can hardly be a poet who has not been influenced by other poets, nor inspired by what has been written before. The issue remains one of whether the poet is able to say something in a way that is new or fresh, and speaks also for the person reading it. As a first collection, *Poems* would have been a record of his development – amongst many other things. But is there a voice emerging that can be called Wilde's?

The further issue is whether Wilde's is a truly authentic poetic voice. If he had written poems entitled 'In the style of ... ' or 'In imitation of ... ' he might have dealt with his fellow students' objections. But he was still young, and anxious to prove himself: hence everything he had written had to be published. This is a weakness shared by poets (young or old) down the ages – for example the poet who says: 'I have five hundred poems that must all be published', and doesn't ask the question 'Are they all worthwhile?' In reality, with few exceptions – Shakespeare's *Sonnets* being one – a large collection sweeping up everything will contain duds.

But consider the concepts of 'imitation', 'being influenced by' and 'plagiarism'. Wilde was accused of all three, and not without foundation. Arising out of consideration of these concepts is the answer to Wilde's authenticity as a poet. Plagiarism is the most serious of these in that it passes off something that is not the author's as his own work. There is some evidence to support this in his poem 'Panthea', which borrows from Roden Noel's *Pan*. Roden Noel (1834–94) was a poet of some distinction as well as popularity, although now undeservedly forgotten. His work would have been well known to Wilde.

Here is Roden Noel:

Ah, Nature, would that I before I pass
Might thrill with joy of thy communion
One childlife only knowing thee from afar!
Love we may well, for surely one were nought
Without the other, intermarrying breath;
Nature the systole, thought the diastole
Of one Divine forever-beating Heart.

And now, Wilde:

> We are resolved into the supreme air,
>   We are made one with what we touch and see,
> With our heart's blood each crimson sun is fair,
>   With our young lives each spring-impassioned tree
> Flames into green, the wildest beasts that range
> The moor our kinsmen are, all life is one, and all is change.
>
> With beat of systole and of diastole
>   One grand great life throbs through earth's giant heart,
> And mighty waves of single Being roll
>   From nerveless germ to man, for we are part
> Of every rock and bird and beast and hill,
> One with the things that prey on us, and one with
>   what we kill …

Not only is this a similarity of theme – understandable – it is after all, a common enough contemporary philosophical theme – but also the similarity of wording suggests at the very least a mental laziness, but more probably a lift of idea and expression from one long poem to be inserted into another. The same theme, with similar expressions crops up in 'Humanitad':

> To make the Body and Spirit one
>   With all right things, till no thing live in vain
> From morn to noon, but in sweet unison
>   With every pulse of flesh and throb of brain
> The Soul in flawless essence high enthroned,
> Against all outer vain attack invincibly bastioned …

But this is philosophical in intention, and there is in philosophy a continual reworking of ideas, and there are relatively few new ideas that actually change the way we think. It may be supposed that Wilde did want to refashion ideas, which makes him more the philosopher than the poet. Without being harsh, there are more than resonances of other men's 'voices', especially in his earlier work. His self-proclaimed genius was not in poetry, and in his reflective moments he knew it. He could also recognise fine contemporary poetry when he read it and was generous in his praise of it.

Looking at *Poems* and the collected poetry – there is sharp division of his work into two: the work which really is written from the heart and which is straightforward, and as a result unaffected, unadorned, sometimes graceful and usually direct both in language and in penetration of the subject matter. The other work, which is often seen as typical 'Wilde', is overtly 'poetical', elaborate and overburdened. It is seen as evidence by his *aficionados* of his being a 'lord of language'. Equally it could be seen as artificial in the sense that it is evasive, designed to charm, and decorative, if the rococo is held to be appealing.

The division in his work between the elaborate, over-fluent and the direct style is evident in a poem such as 'Requiescat' which from external evidence, cannot be anything other than written from grief over his little sister's childhood death, when viewed alongside other, especially the longer, poems. The style of 'Requiescat' is simple – the words are Anglo-Saxon rather than Latin-based … : 'Heap earth upon it.' Even without knowledge of its reference, it would be difficult not to be moved. 'Requiescat' was modelled on Matthew Arnold's poem of the same name, but at the same time is different from it. This is closer to the mature Wilde – influenced by what he read and selecting from it, but using that eclecticism for his own purpose. Similarly, the poem he wrote about the death of his father 'The True Knowledge', 'Thou knowest all … ', is written in plain language and is a true note of reverence and loss.

By way of contrast, the longer poems, for example 'Ravenna', the Newdigate Prize poem, read more as exercises in conventional symbols (for example the role of England, with conventional attitudes) and with academic language to match. This is not Wilde in control of his material or theme – except in the sense of playing at writing. It cannot be described as authentic or poetry that is anything other than conventional – although it is readable. Again, by contrast, a light-hearted and admittedly lightweight poem, 'The Little Ship' also uses language simply (as does 'Requiescat') – and expresses sentiments that are common-place, that are readily grasped:

Have you forgotten the ship love
I made as a childish toy,
When you were a little girl love,
And I was a little boy? ...

I carved a wonderful mast love
From my Father's Sunday stick,
You cut up your one good dress love
That the sail should be of silk.

The capacity to speak directly is there and is apposite. This straightforwardness of expression is found in nearly all of Wilde's shorter poems and where it is, it is effective. It finally re-emerges with force in *The Ballad of Reading Gaol*. Influenced by, imitative of – but ceasing to plagiarise, uneven; perhaps we can hear a distinctive voice emerging.

Wilde's poetry falls, historically, between two ages – the mid-Victorian and a much later age – the early 20th century and the Imagists. In his Victorian mode – lacking the vigour of Clough (but sharing some of his wit), he is capable of something of the sweetness of Tennyson and, of course, the perverse *longueurs* of Swinburne, as can be seen in *The Sphinx*. Other longer poems such as 'Humanitad' and 'Panthea' veer between Tennyson and Swinburne in style. They are characteristically mellifluous, perhaps almost anaesthetic in their effect. They take themselves seriously and are overworked 'poetical' verse, and suffer as a result. In his simpler, more original mode his verse anticipates the

Imagists and is straightforward, for example 'Symphony in Yellow' – but it is precisely where his verse is straightforward that his voice is to be found, unfettered by pretension, nor seemingly caring to be 'poetical'. He has been rediscovered lately as a poet of the 'Decadence', whereas poetry anthologies of the self-conscious '1890s' struggled with the dates of his poems.

Wilde's facility with language made composition relatively easy – and he was able to write work which is still readable. But poetry was changing – under the influence of Edgar Allan Poe:

> I hold that a long poem does not exist. I maintain that the phrase 'a long poem' is simply a flat contradiction in terms.
>
> I need scarcely observe that a poem deserves its title only inasmuch as it excites, by elevating the soul. The value of the poem is in ratio of this elevating excitement. But all excitements are through a psychal necessity, transient. That degree of excitement which would entitle a poem to be so called at all, cannot be sustained throughout a composition of any length. (*Poetic Principle*)

Long poems lacked the 'vital requisite in all works of Art, Unity'. Logically, Poe then viewed *Paradise Lost* 'as a series of minor poems' and *The Iliad* as 'a series of lyrics'. Whatever the merits of Poe's argument in general, they have an application to Wilde's poetry: on the one hand he felt it necessary to compose long poems – whether for a prize ('Ravenna') or because he had sufficient facility of expression to lead him to believe that he could. This tendency affects poets even in the modern age: it is seen as a challenge – which leads to spinning things out, the use or misuse of metaphor. These are observable in Wilde's longer poems – but less so in *The Sphinx* and *The Ballad of Reading Gaol.*

Wilde's longer poems, except *The Ballad of Reading Gaol*, do not seriously rank with the best of his age. The issue is not their derivativeness but that fire which makes poetry what it is. His shorter poems are intrinsically more interesting, but again some lack the edge that would be implied by their subject matter. For example 'Ave Imperatrix', which might have been a powerful protest against that contemporary imperialism that wasted the youth of England on pointless foreign adventures or in the pursuit of profit, is strangely inert. As it happens, one of the references is to Afghanistan. The expression of grief and loss that would have been all too real is somehow not persuasive:

> In vain the laughing girl will lean
> To greet her love with love-lit eyes:
> Down in some treacherous black ravine,
> Clutching his flag, the dead boy lies.

Partly because it is formulaic – 'laughing girl' and later:

> Pale women who have lost their lord
> Will kiss the relics of the slain –
> Some tarnished epaulette – some sword –
> Poor toys to soothe such anguished pain.

'Pale women' and 'their lord' seem to be stock phrases, which reduce the potential force of 'tarnished epaulette' whilst 'poor toys' make the verse seem less forceful, more equivocal than not. The poem closes by looking to the day when a 'young Republic like a sun/Rise from these crimson seas of war'. This appears facile: it is a measure of the poem falling below its mark – and it does this because of a lack of passion, which flows into a lack of poetic force and structure.

Thinking about his public verse he appears ambivalent. In the 'Sonnet to Liberty', whilst understanding the cry for liberty, he has reservations about the mindset of these freedom fighters: the children of liberty ' … whose dull eyes/See nothing save their own unlovely woe/Whose minds know nothing, nothing care to know … '; he foresees them leading on to a kind of tyranny – an idea that he explores further in 'The Soul of Man under Socialism'. The liberty he is interested in is something different – the freedom to be, and to do: it is quite a fine distinction but important, hence

Rob nations of their rights inviolate
And I remain unmoved – and yet, and yet,
These Christs that die upon the barricades,
God knows it I am with them, in some things.

When it comes to revolution and the sympathy that might have naturally come to Wilde – one might think of Speranza and the revolutions that had spread across Europe in 1848 – we find the phrase: ' … I am with them, in some things.' Ambivalence is an aspect of Wilde – did he know? It might be supposed that he did not.

His passion becomes evident when the subject matter is personal rather than public or political. When he considers the nature of love – and the homoerotic theme is remarkably clear – he becomes moved, and definite. In 'Glukipikros Eros' usually translated as 'Bittersweet Love' which is from Sappho (Fragment 40, Bergk's numbering). Wharton translates this as:

Now Love masters my limbs and shakes me, fatal creature,
bitter sweet.

Sappho's expression of impossible love unfulfilled enables Wilde to write about the parting of lovers, and the sweetness and bitterness of love:

Sweet, I blame you not, for mine the fault was,
    had I not been made of common clay
I had climbed the higher heights unclimbed yet,
    seen the fuller air, the larger day.

He speculates about the love he would have had which is symbolised by Keats:

Keats had lifted up his hymeneal curls from out
    the poppy-seeded wine,
With ambrosial mouth had kissed my forehead, clasped
    the hand of noble love in mine …

and later:

… Two young lovers lying in an orchard would have read
    the story of our love.

Would have read the legend of my passion,
    known the bitter secret of my heart,
Kissed as we have kissed, but never parted as we two
    are fated now to part …

Straightforward but resigned:

Yet I am not sorry that I loved you – ah! what else
    had I a boy to do, –

he ends the poem defiantly, and truthfully:

I have made my choice, have lived my poems, and,
   though youth has gone in wasted days,
I have found the lover's crown of myrtle better than
   the poet's crown of bays.

The power of passion – 'I … have lived my poems' – is self-evident in these lines.

The symbol of Keats occurs again in 'On the Sale by Auction of Keats' Love Letters': the poet is the male emblem of love, a martyr to love, and his letters are surrounded 'by the brawlers of the auction mart' – the sense of outrage is palpable.

Some of his shorter poems were influenced significantly, by French writers, in particular Baudelaire and Verlaine. They were the antidote to Wilde's Greek learning which resonated for Wilde, as with other late Victorians, reinforcing their sympathy with Keats and his work. Whistler's influence, both in choice of titles and themes – can also be felt: 'Impressions: La Fuite de la Lune' and more especially in 'Impression du Matin' and 'Symphony in Yellow', both of which refer to Whistler's 'Symphony in Grey'. They can be read too as a coda to Wordsworth's 'Composed upon Westminster Bridge, September 3, 1802':

… This City now doth, like a garment, wear
The beauty of the morning: silent, bare,
Ships, towers, domes, theatres, and temples lie
Open unto the fields, and to the sky;
All bright and glittering in the smokeless air.

'Impression du Matin', Wilde:

> ... A barge with ochre-coloured hay
> Dropt from the wharf: and chill and cold
>
> The yellow fog came creeping down
>   The bridges, till the houses' walls
>   Seemed changed to shadows and St Paul's
> Loomed like a bubble o'er the town ...

The poem denotes a shift of temperament from the Wordsworthian Romantic, optimistic to the Decadent, which is signalled by its imagery, but underscored, unnecessarily by its closing verse:

> ... But one pale woman all alone,
> The daylight kissing her wan hair,
> Loitered beneath the gas lamps' flare,
> With lips of flame and heart of stone.

In 'Symphony in Yellow' Wilde reworks the same theme:

> An omnibus across the bridge
> Crawls like a yellow butterfly,
> And, here and there, a passer-by
> Shows like a little restless midge.
>
> Big barges full of yellow hay
> Are moored against the shadowy wharf,
> And, like a yellow silken scarf,
> The thick fog hangs along the quay

The yellow leaves begin to fade
And flutter from the Temple elms,
And at my feet the pale green Thames
Lies like a rod of rippled jade.

It shows greater fluency and is freer in its composition, not only in the near-rhymes of 'hay' with 'quay' and 'wharf' with 'scarf', but also in its absence of drama. There is no need to place a prostitute in the final lines to make a point about the change of perspective: the 'rod of rippled jade' as a simile for the Thames, does this.

In certain respects these poems anticipate the Imagism of the early 20th century. They work as poems, because their language is clear – but not unsubtle – but above all there is something to be said, where the manner in which it is said, and its content, work together. The issue for Wilde, surprisingly, is control over his work – it is too easy to find a pretty phrase in otherwise strong work: in 'Les Ballons' ('Fantaisies Décoratives')

Against these turbid turquoise skies
The light and luminous balloons
Dip and drift like satin moons,
Drift like silken butterflies;

the similes of balloons become 'dancing girls', then 'strange transparent pearls', 'silver dust' and then 'thin globes of amethyst' and 'wandering opals keeping tryst/With the rubies of the lime'.

Wilde's skills in composition can be seen in 'Theocritus: A Villanelle', which demonstrates his facility with metre and language:

> O singer of Persephone!
> In the dim meadows desolate
> Dost thou remember Sicily?

but raises the question of whether this rises above an exercise in technique.

On the self, sex, love and lust Wilde has something to say – there is an existential tension in his verse as can be seen in 'Hélas':

> To drift with every passion till my soul
> Is a stringed lute on which all winds can play,
> Is it for this that I have given away
> Mine ancient wisdom, and austere control? …
>
>   … Lo! With a little rod
> I did but touch the honey of romance –
> And must I lose a soul's inheritance?

'The Harlot's House' brings these themes together, and uses the verse form to develop an idea in a way that is dramatic, telling a story of the battle between love and lust:

We caught the tread of dancing feet,
We loitered down the moonlit street,
And stopped beneath the harlot's house …

… Sometimes a clockwork puppet pressed
A phantom lover to her breast,
Sometimes they seemed to try to sing.

This directness and even spare use of language is not seen again until *The Ballad of Reading Gaol*, which uses some of the same images. Wilde, if accused of plagiarising the work of others, relentlessly reused his own. Both poems have a moral point to make, and both suffer when the language becomes over-elaborate and the theme self– consciously 'poetic'.

The Sphinx

The Sphinx was the last poem that Wilde published in the style of his early, longer poems. The obvious reason for this is that he began the poem at the start of his career and, with the help of a rhyming dictionary, completed it in the 1890s. It has an internal rhyme which it uses to beguile the reader whilst evoking fabulous and sensuous images. It uses the image and presence of a domestic cat (the sphinx which with its asexuality is a symbol of decadence) who is imagined to have lived fantastically through the pagan as well as Christian centuries – and who is commanded:

> Lift up your large black satin eyes which are like
>   cushions where one sinks!
> Fawn at my feet, fantastic Sphinx! And sing me
>   all your memories!

The poem is thus apparently an extended whimsy, or conceit – where the battle is between sense and the music of language, Pater's 'All art aspires to the condition of music.' Yet it exhibits control over its material. The poem's 'music' represents the cat's sinuous presence whilst surveying the physicality and passions of lives lived described with rich, sensual imagery. The poet tires, finally of the pageant and of the cat: 'Why are you tarrying? Get hence! I weary of your sullen ways', projecting the poet's guilt on to it:

> Get hence, you loathsome mystery! Hideous
>   animal, get hence!
> You wake in me each bestial sense, you make me
>   what I would not be.

The poet rejects the cat but admits that 'you make my creed a barren sham' whilst taking refuge, ambiguously in the Christian faith – where Christ is referred to as the crucifix's 'pallid burden' (a reference to Swinburne's anti-Christian 'pale Galilean') who ' weeps for every soul that dies, and weeps for every soul in vain'. Paganism is sensual but empty and Christianity ineffective, at the very least, for him – the conceit is unravelled and the whimsy found to be despairing.

The Ballad of Reading Gaol

The *Ballad* was the last of Wilde's creative work. It arose because he needed to say something, in a way that would reach a reading public, about his misery and humiliation whilst drawing more from that experience – significantly the suffering of others. He needed to say something about how love and betrayal brought about the destruction of a life. Bosie's betrayal of his love (if we are to take the text of *De Profundis* at face value) led to his destruction as a social figure – it is typified by, and justified by the refrain 'Each man kills the thing he loves'. In his turn, it could be said that Wilde had betrayed his mother (after Wilde's trials she did not care to go out of her house and died heartbroken in 1896) and ruined Constance's life. Wilde had become like his father – which he did not wish to be.

Wilde's crime and guilt is projected onto a fellow prisoner, a guardsman, condemned to be executed for the murder of his wife. 'The coward does it with a kiss' (Judas/Bosie; Wilde/Constance/Lady Wilde), 'the brave man with a sword' (the guardsman). At the same time it is Wilde's anatomisation of his own failure – his betrayal of his mother's love, and its consequence, her death. Post-prison he reached out to Constance, the one remaining guarantee of love. In settling for Bosie, superficially available, he destroyed her love, again. This is to dwell on external evidence. Internally it is clear that the poem expresses his anguish and remorse. It also frees him from those things. He needed to write the poem: it is not finally the product of an attitude nor is it an aspect of a pose. And if that were not enough, being able to see through the illusion of social station, to humanity, to its common sufferings was granted to him. Another outpouring of this enlightenment was the two letters he wrote to newspapers about prison conditions. The *Ballad* may not be a 'perfect' poem in the sense that flaws can be pointed out, but it is authentic poetry. It works and it has an expressive power that is not evident in so much else of his poetry. The aspect of Wilde it showed is not one with which the world at large was (and is) familiar – the wit and Dandy – but what lay beneath the elaborate social veneer of his persona, the reasoning but provocative humanitarian.

His mode of composition was chosen on the ground that it represented the common experience. The form of public lament traditional in writings about prison is the form of the ballad, a tale with enough dramatic force to carry the argument through to its conclusion. His model, and he worked as he always did by using a model – was that given by the uncommon, Coleridge in the 'The Rime of the Ancient Mariner'. There is also the influence of Housman – the simplicity of language which is stretched to its limits, characteristic of Housman especially and also of Wilde when he is under pressure to say something. Housman's influence is evident from the meditation on the hanging of a man in poem IX of *A Shropshire Lad*:

And naked to the hangman's noose
The morning clocks will ring
A neck God made for other use
Than strangling in a string

And sharp the link of life will snap
And dead on air will stand …

… So here I'll watch the night and wait
To see the morning shine,
And he will hear the stroke of eight
And not the stroke of nine.

And as Anthony Daniels says in the *New Criterion* March 2014, ' … the echoes in Wilde's poem are obvious':

But it is not sweet with nimble feet
To dance upon the air …

We waited for the stroke of eight
Each tongue was thick with thirst.

The poem is all of these things and also more: it is a protest against the truly medieval conditions imposed on prisoners by the Victorians. Decency of public provision, like the conduct of wars conceived by generals, is usually on the basis of ideas that are no longer – if ever they were – suited to the needs of the actual society of men or the task in hand.

The two strands of Wilde's creativity: the direct voice

driven by living; and the decorative/musical voice; come together in this poem. This is typical of Wilde's work – but in respect of the *Ballad* it is seen as a compositional flaw.

The narrative is straight to the point. It opens in the prison yard with the prisoners on their daily exercise. The focus is on the man who had murdered his wife and is to suffer death by hanging: '*That fellow's got to swing.*' The language used is direct but, as in all of Wilde's work, unmistakably coloured, yet also restrained, not florid nor windy, and thus all the more effective:

> He did not wear his scarlet coat,
>   For blood and wine are red,
> And blood and wine were on his hands
>   When they found him with the dead,
> The poor dead woman whom he loved,
>   And murdered in her bed.

The scarlet coat was the uniform of the British army guardsmen of the day (soldiers were popularly known as 'redcoats').

The shock of discovering that the guardsman is sentenced to death is registered when 'the very prison walls/Suddenly seemed to reel', which is neat transposition of feeling onto things. Wilde's analysis of the guardsman's crime is introduced: 'Yet each man kills the thing he loves'; they simply kill in different ways, 'The brave man with a sword' – but only he is punished ritualistically, humiliatingly

– kept from suicide so that he can be hanged, accompanied by the 'shivering Chaplain robed in white,/The Sheriff stern with gloom,/And the Governor all in shiny black,/With the yellow face of Doom … ', which is ironic.

It requires suspension of potential disbelief in the thesis – which, as is usual with Wilde, takes the counter-argument into the camp of the conventional.

Section 2 reflects further on the insouciance of the guardsman as he awaits the day of his execution, indifferent to the helplessness of his situation. The poet is the one who feels the horror of the outcome. And the parallel is also with the poet – who empathises with the guardsman – 'two outcast men we were:/The world had thrust us from its heart,/And God from out His care.' The poet later in the poem comes to the opposite view, but by means of suffering.

Section 3 uses the images of the prison – the fact of the roles of the Governor, Doctor and Chaplain and how their meaning is voided by their actions:

> The Governor was strong upon
> The Regulations Act:
> The Doctor said that Death was but
> A scientific fact:
> And twice a day the Chaplain called,
> And left a little tract.

'Tract' means a religious tract, designed to convert the faithless, and was popular in Victorian Britain. This is biting satire – worthy of Juvenal: the Chaplain might have been expected to extend the hand of kindness, the Governor to exercise his governance humanely, and the Doctor to be healer, which is patently not the case.

In this section there are two passages that cause critics difficulty: the first which introduces ghosts that patrol the corridors and sing ghoulishly – surely here Wilde is over-influenced by Coleridge's ballad – and together with cocks crowing – which is redolent of Peter's betrayal of Christ – the effect verges on the melodramatic. This must be contrasted with the power of the closing part of the section where all the prisoners are affected by the time of the execution – 'And from all the gaol rose up a wail/Of impotent despair', and the scream of the hanged man.

The poet projects from himself onto the guardsman and then back to himself. He is trying to understand what he has done (sin) what the consequences are (punishment) whilst at the same time wondering about its justice. Wilde had lived two lives:

> … And the wild regrets, and the bloody sweats,
>   None know so well as I:
> For he who lives more lives than one
>   More deaths than one must die.

Section 4 resumes the pace of the first two stanzas and has little that might be described as elaboration. The claustrophobic nature of imprisonment, restraint, with no freedom, no ordinary choices:

> So they kept us close till nigh on noon,
>   And then they rang the bell,
> And the Warders with their jingling keys
>   Opened each listening cell,
> And down the iron stair we tramped,
>   Each from his separate Hell.

This is followed by reflecting on the issue of legal justice: if the sin is the same – killing the thing we love – why is not the punishment the same as the guardsman's? This may be stretching a metaphor too far, but this is the point: 'let him who has no sin cast the first stone … ' Wilde wanted to explain it further –

> But there were those amongst us all
>   Who walked with downcast head,
> And knew that, had each got his due,
>   They should have died instead:
> He had but killed a thing that lived,
>   Whilst they had killed the dead.

It does not quite work. What does work is the sense of imprisonment, despair at the human condition – which easily becomes bestial:

> The Warders strutted up and down,
>   And watched their herd of brutes …

It is marred at certain stages by the merely decorative. Some might say the poetaster in Wilde took over, where he imagines the murderer's remains not being tainted but giving life to more vivid flowers:

> And the red rose would but blow more red,
>   The white rose whiter blow.
>
> Out of his mouth a red, red rose!
>   Out of his heart a white!

That is unfair: it is a minor flaw and giving an excuse to those who do not wish to take Wilde seriously as a poet and to dismiss the poem. That would be wrong, but it would be true to say that the poem suffers from a too slavish adherence to the form of 'The Rime of the Ancient Mariner' and thus a lapse into Wilde's familiar ways of composition. Whatever the poetic disadvantages of this strategy, the negative effect is neutralised by the closing lines of this section. These lines resonate, and are also emblematic of Wilde's situation:

> Yet all is well; he has but passed
>   To Life's appointed bourne:
> And alien tears will fill for him
>   Pity's long-broken urn,
> For his mourners will be outcast men
>   And outcasts always mourn.

Section 5 deals with any frailty of argument there might be with a statement of Wilde's antinomian position: 'I know not whether Laws be right,/Or whether Laws be wrong'; it is the necessity of law that is wrong, and once established, it perpetuates that wrongdoing via the institutions of punishment and prison:

> The vilest deeds like poison weeds,
>   Bloom well in prison-air;
> It is only what is good in Man
>   That wastes and withers there ...

The poet looks in despair for succour and finds it divine mercy:

> ... God's eternal Laws are kind
>   And break the heart of stone ...

and in the person of Christ:

> ' ... How else but through a broken heart
>   May Lord Christ enter in?'

The hanged man

> ' ... Waits for the holy hands that took
>   The Thief to Paradise ...

The poem ends, as it begins, with the assertion that each man kills the thing he loves, some with flattery or a kiss, 'The brave man with a sword!'.

Note how throughout, the bitter experience of prison, wrongdoing and its consequences are evoked by simple words, so that poetry is made – not 'poetically' but by the force of feeling:

> But each man's heart beat thick and quick.

The words and phrases represent prison, its harsh routines:

> With slouch and swing around the ring
>   We trod the Fools' Parade

and the perfunctory nature of officialdom. This, in all its codified pettiness, is oppression and cruelty.

Comparison with 'popular' poets of his day, for example Frederick Locker-Lampson and Sir William Watson, will show why they are justly forgotten, and why Wilde is deservedly still read.

Wilde's longer poems suggest a serious philosophical purpose which resonates throughout his work, even if they do not always work as poetry. Leaving that aside, competence and fluency with language does on its own not make a poet, and he could certainly write. Importantly, he cared about and loved poetry: he knew what it *is*. His critical faculty made him acutely aware that his own work did not always measure up to that of others (and he said so): Baudelaire, Verlaine, Francis Thompson's *The Hound of Heaven*, Housman's *A Shropshire Lad*. He may not have succeeded if judged by his own private high standards, but he did not fail either. When he was not self-consciously the 'poet', and this was when he had something needful to say that grew from him, 'it' dictated his verse – he became what he most sought to be: a poet.

4

Essays and Criticism

INTENTIONS, WILDE'S SKETCHES OF THE development of his thought, was brought together from prior publication in journals, and published in 1891 one month after the publication of *Dorian Gray*, but prior to his successful plays. It cannot be doubted that his group of essays, 'The Decay of Lying', 'Pen, Pencil and Poison', 'The Critic as Artist' and 'The Truth of Masks', was meant to be provocative. Wilde was endeavouring to make clear his views of art and society as well as philosophy. Although separately composed, they work as a whole: the title *Intentions* is accurate, except in one case: 'Pen, Pencil and Poison', which is complete in itself.

As remarked before, he looked for models, if not paradigms, of his discoveries, not only in his modes of expression, as was his wont, but in how life is to be lived.

Blend art and life if you will, but life is to be lived and to the full, and art is the way in which this is best understood. Of the four essays, two, 'The Decay of Lying' and 'The Critic as Artist' take the form of a dialogue between two leisured but educated young men. The model of the dialogue is Plato's and Greek more generally, both in its homoerotic and intellectual senses. In 'The Critic' he seeks to justify this choice by reference to historical antecedents. As in the later works of Plato, the conversation is not between equals but rather one of an intellectual preacher being prompted by his somewhat awestruck listener. To this extent, the dialogues feel lifeless, especially by comparison with what Wilde finally achieved with his plays for the commercial theatre.

Wilde followed Arnold (and he acknowledges the debt), whose strange, brooding presence influenced so much of late Victorian England's intellectual élite. Arnold's essay 'The Function of Criticism at the Present Time', in *Essays in Criticism* (1865), makes the critic's role a creative one:

> ... Again, judging is often spoken of as the critic's one business, and so in some sense it is; but the judgement which almost insensibly forms itself in a fair and clear mind, along with fresh knowledge, must be the critic's great concern for himself. And it is by communicating fresh knowledge ... as a sort of companion and clue, not as an abstract lawgiver, – that the critic will generally do most good to his readers ...

Did Wilde add much to this? In entitling his book *Intentions* he paid homage to Pater's *Appreciations* (an altogether fuller work than Wilde's essays). But Wilde differed from either: he tried to live what he wrote. Art was an adventure in life as much as anything else. And his ambisexuality was an aspect of this. Society can never, in any age, permit real freedom of expression in life – there are always social conventions that prohibit it. Wilde's works might thus seem flawed. But given that these are social conventions, his triumph artistically was to use them both to expose and to express their hypocrisy, and to express something else altogether. This is most clearly to be seen in *The Importance of Being Earnest* and *The Ballad of Reading Gaol*, and the roots of it are in *Intentions* and, in another way, again in 'The Soul of Man under Socialism'.

'The Decay of Lying'

'The Decay of Lying' is ostensibly about the function of art, and is a restatement of Wilde's views when he was seen as the apostle of aestheticism: 'Art never expresses anything but itself … it develops purely on its own lines … ' The doctrine of art for art's sake originated with Théophile Gautier (1811–72), in the preface of his novel *Mademoiselle de Maupin* (1836). 'All bad art comes from returning to Life and Nature, and elevating them into ideals.' Wilde's anti-realist stance is justified by the fact that novels and art forms that are focused on the fashions and manners of a particular time rapidly date. He would prefer the fantastic to the dullness of Zola, and even his beloved Balzac has to be rescued from possible censure: his was an 'imaginative reality':

> Champing his gilded oats, the Hippogriff will stand in our stalls, and over our heads will float the Blue Bird singing of beautiful and impossible things, of things that are lovely and that never happen, of things that are not and that should be.

This is the spirit of decadence, distilled to a sentence, most obviously, but more importantly it is the quest for that which is timeless – the expression of a truth that stands the test of time, not mere facts that mutate with the passing of days. It is also a declaration – a wish for the world as we should like it to be. Herein lies some of Wilde's enduring appeal. His dictum 'Life imitates Art … ' which results from ' … the fact that the self-conscious aim of Life is to find expression, and … Art offers it certain beautiful forms through which it may realise that energy' is a muddle, but an inspired one, resting on definitions of life, art and nature that are flexible. Wilde did not, self-confessedly, see the merits of consistency. There is an effect due to these broad brush marks. Nature also imitates Art. The explanation of this assertion lies in Pater and, prior to him, Kant. This neo-Kantianism holds that it is the operation of the mind that produces all the effects of nature, i.e. space, time, physical characteristics. It is not possible for us to comprehend nature except through these categories, which are 'mental' in origin. Wilde's assertion takes this to its logical (and unintended) conclusion: ' ... the only effects that she [Nature] can show us are effects that we have already seen through poetry, or in paintings ... ' This works in a number of ways: as a critique of the empiricism still prevalent in Anglo-American philosophy that holds that 'experience' of nature is the validation of truth – 'facts' which Wilde so despised – and also that the mind is a blank sheet of paper, a *tabula rasa* on which Nature writes. It can also de-humanise – what we choose to focus on can become exclusive, self-validating and thus wrong.

'The final revelation is that Lying, the telling of beautiful untrue things, is the proper aim of Art ... ' This calculated provocation rests on the notions of 'beautiful' and 'untrue'. To talk of, or represent, 'ugly' things is not 'art' – but what is beautiful, and what ugly? Wilde is writing of fiction as well – and referring to a vital function of art, which is to explore all that is possible: ' ... the basis of life. The energy of life ... is simply the desire for expression, and art is always presenting various forms through which this expression can be attained.' Consistent at least, but repetitive: layer upon layer of rhetoric, tone of voice, to persuade. He very nearly succeeds.

The incompleteness of his thought is both frustrating and seductive. When reduced to its elements, though quotable it is not truly inspired writing – the gap is fatally between his thoughts and his chosen mode of expression.

'Pen, Pencil and Poison'

By contrast, this little essay, brought about by reviewing a biography of Thomas Wainewright, is complete and lives as a work of art. If this is all we know of Wainewright it is sufficient. Wilde was enabled to enter the character of this poisoner and forger, and to *understand* him, yet was able to discuss the difference between his own projection and that personality. Wainewright was drawn to the forbidden – because he found fulfilment in it, and he was a lover of art, a prototype aesthete also 'fascinated by this strange sin ... ' where ' ... he sought to find expression by pen or poison.' Wainewright escaped arrest for forgery, to France, to return to England, having followed a woman he loved, thereby ' ... imperilling his life. Yet he returned. Should one wonder? It was said that the woman was very beautiful. Besides, she did not love him.' The Wildean analysis of life and art is all there – Wainewright's sins could be overlooked (' ... the fact of a man being a poisoner is nothing against his prose'), risking his freedom for an impossible love, and Wainewright's artistic achievement requiring time to form a judgement since he put living his life before all else.

This essay may be counted as one of Wilde's successes – regretfully little regarded – written under the pressure of meaning, unencumbered with ideas that merely strike a posture. It is not a confection, although it might appear as such. It is a profound analysis, more than rational in that it comprehends the irrational in lives as they are lived. Wainewright is depicted as a man of great aesthetic sympathies and critical acumen, and an artist, also a 'writer of capital prose', obsessed with sin which is a driving force, and destroyed by a love that is not returned. There is a fatalism about Wilde's self-actualisation – things are as they are and could not otherwise be, and there is too a perverse desire to surrender to that fate. This formula 'find out what you are then be it' is intellectually tough (well, who exactly are you?) and emotionally demanding (can you live this through?); nor is it just about people's sex lives or art on its own, but lives and the world they are lived in. It is an expression of a continuing theme of Wilde's: that of the individual.

If the essay contains unpalatable truths, it was meant to. Reconciliation of good and evil, if there is any, is to be found in the artistic individual.

'The Critic as Artist'

Compared to 'Pen, Pencil and Poison' this essay seems overlengthy and artificial. The projection of Wilde's thought onto a dialogue between two young, wealthy men, is little more than a device. Dramatically, the dialogue works better than in 'The Decay of Lying', but that is not claiming a great deal. The dialogue is divided into two parts, one prior and the other subsequent to supper, in the same locale, thus maintaining some notion of a dramatic unity. Behind though, lies Wilde's overturning of conventional wisdom as expressed by Samuel Johnson:

> Criticism is a study by which men grow important and formidable at a very small expense. The power of invention has been conferred by Nature upon few ... but every man can exert such judgment as he has upon the works of others; and he whom Nature has made weak, and Idleness keeps ignorant, may yet support his vanity by the name of a Critick.

What better than to make the critic central to Art?

Part I asserts the necessity of art criticism to the attainment of enduring art. Criticism is a creative contribution along the lines proposed, as we have seen, by Arnold. It helps make up the intellectual climate in which great art can flourish: that must be true even though we may have no direct evidence for it as, say, in the time of the ancients. This does not appear, now, so contentious, but is the critic an artist? Certainly not, in the sense that the creative initiating artist is. It seems to be a second-order activity, and Wilde's somewhat contentious assessments of contemporary (19th-century) writers, however well expressed, confirm this.

When he refers to Browning he says:

Yes, Browning was great. And as what will he be remembered? As a poet? Ah, not as a poet! ... as a writer of fiction, as the most supreme writer of fiction ... Considered from the point of view of a creator of character he ranks next to him who made *Hamlet* ... The only man who can touch the hem of his garment is George Meredith. Meredith is a prose Browning, and so is Browning. He used poetry as a medium for writing in prose.

It is characteristic of Wilde's critical audiences down the years, that they seize the apophthegm 'Meredith is a prose Browning, and so is Browning ... ' both to distance themselves from the opinion and not to consider what Wilde is actually saying. He would complain, at the end of his creative life, that he was misunderstood. It is the art of disclosure, the better to effect concealment: in satisfying all, he risks satisfying none. And he is remembered for his asides – deemed to be more apposite than his main themes: hence 'modern journalism ... justifies its own existence by the great Darwinian principle of the survival of the vulgarest.' The difference between literature and journalism is: 'journalism is unreadable and literature is not read.' Note the subtle shifts of mean of 'read'. That is, finally, a poet's gift.

In relation to art and life, Wilde reiterates the vital interplay between the two: he revisits Plato, pointing out a dilemma which resonates throughout Wilde's own work:

The problems of idealism and realism, as he [Plato] sets them forth, may seem to many to be somewhat barren of result in the metaphysical sphere of abstract being in which he places them, but transfer them to the sphere of art, and you will find that they are still vital and full of meaning.

If any single statement sums up Wilde's strategy – whether for stories, or drama, this would be it.

He has framed the discussion with Aristotle, and he returns to him:

... taking Tragedy, for instance, and investigating the material it uses, which is language, its subject matter which is life, the method by which it works, which is action, the conditions under which it reveals itself, which are those of theatric presentation, its logical structure, which is plot, and its final aesthetic appeal which is to the sense of beauty realised through the passions of pity and awe.

This is serious analysis – but the meaning of beauty has shifted from its commonplace sense. The argument is driven into life: health and healthy functions reside in energy, which must be expressed: 'to have a capacity for a passion and not to realise it, is to make oneself incomplete and limited.' This leads to the individual again: 'it is not the moment that makes the man, but the man who creates the age.' Even myth may be the 'invention of one single mind'.

Christ, Mohammed or the Buddha might be instanced

in support of what appears to be a contentious claim. At the same time the vision is deterministic, almost fatalistic: the only choice is whether or not to realise a passion. Outcomes are somewhat of a lottery – a good person might be repelled by the consequences of their actions, whilst the wicked might achieve something worthwhile. Wilde is inclined to assert the primacy of sin and the sinner in the progress of the world.

We do not see these things because men 'are the slaves of words', although he might here mean ideas: 'they rage against Materialism, as they call it, forgetting that there has been no material improvement that has not spiritualised the world.' He went further. So-called 'spiritual awakenings … have … wasted the world's faculties in barren hopes … fruitless aspirations … empty or trammelling creeds.' Thus what we call 'sin is an essential element of progress'. Basically, life would be dull and stagnant without it. A similar enough argument though was put forward by Mandeville in the *Spirit of the Hive*. A radical set of thoughts, but they need more than excitement to maintain them.

This is the setting to which art criticism belongs, it challenges and reshapes perceptions as much as original works of art: it cannot be castigated because it borrows the forms of original art: that is precisely its merit. Criticism might suggest ideas in a work of art that are in fact far from the artist's mind. This is a difficult tightrope to walk since it is the reverse of the arguments put forward in 'The Decay of Lying'. Criticism is both 'independent' (as in a work of art) and 'the record of one's soul'. In other words, all roads lead to the individual – perhaps with a capital 'I'.

This philosophising carries with it the danger of being an intellectual, emotional and humanistic dead-end, compatible with the destruction of the values that might be held to underpin it. It is true that great art has emerged from disaster and chaos – as Harry Lime in Orson Welles' film *The Third Man* is made to say, which is contrasted with hundreds of years of peace, harmony and brotherly love in Switzerland, which produced 'the cuckoo clock'. It is hard to view the history of the 20th century and not to see the limitation of this – what great art did Germany produce ruled by Hitler, or Russia controlled by Stalin? The extinction of millions of human beings led to misery and that to more misery. The capacity of human beings to suffer may be marvelled at, more than the capacity of those to tyrannise. In 'The Soul of Man under Socialism' Wilde endeavours to deal with a broader picture.

Wilde's wilful love of paradox, exemplified throughout his work is, though, an endeavour to reach the truth, no matter what it may be. Wilde's approach was influenced heavily by Greek thought and rests on the proposition that from contradiction anything follows, but behind contradictions there are truths, which we should constantly seek.

Part II, 'With some remarks upon the importance of discussing everything', endeavours to round off the discussion with more bombardment of ideas and paradigms. It is hard to resist the notion that the defence of the critic has overreached itself. The critic is more than an interpreter of the work of art: he may seek to deepen the mystery surrounding it, and its author. A better appreciation of art arises through studying critics of it. The critic may on occasion be an actor, who acts the play. Wilde was not consistent on this point either – referring elsewhere to actors as 'mimes' or a musician playing a work of Beethoven: they bring their own individuality to the interpretation.

Art is contrasted with life – and life is found wanting. Art is put forward as being self-sufficient, as the unapproachable medium of experience and contemplation. Art is immoral because 'emotion for the sake of emotion is the aim of art, and emotion for the sake of action is the aim of life … Society … is the beginning and basis of morals … Society often forgives the criminal; it never forgives the dreamer.' Wilde then advocates the contemplative life. The contemplative life is focused on the concrete, the actual, and is the substitute for metaphysics and formal religion; and, as it were, to realise this potential there has to be a 'critical spirit'. We would conclude from Wilde's arguments that he believed that art was amoral – outside of morals. He does however except those arts which endeavour to persuade us to action. Drawing distinctions, again, between art and life is difficult: but Wilde's point is always the same: think beyond categories, open your eyes, cultivate yourself by every means available.

Finally, he returns to Arnold, and speaks briefly of education:

> We, in our educational system, have burdened the memory with a load of unconnected facts, and laboriously striven to impart our laboriously acquired knowledge. We teach people how to remember, we never teach them how to grow.

This could be reiterated with benefit today in an epoch where governments believe that education is the absorption of 'drills'. And he makes clear that this critical spirit, with its concentration on the specific work of art, makes culture possible, in ways that are superior to appeals to free markets; and culture makes us cosmopolitan, which renders war itself unnecessary. In an age where free market philosophy is again triumphant (perhaps money-making is, in every age) his voice might be heeded. Criticism has also a sense of detachment, vital to enquiry, 'recognising no position as final '

His excursions into literary criticism illustrate his assertions and, it has to be said, it is these, rather than his general thesis about criticism, that are remembered. On Kipling he says: 'he is our first authority on the second-rate, and has seen marvellous things through keyholes … ' This dialogue practically staggers under the weight of allusion and example, yet there is an earnestness which contrasts with his apparently luxuriously paced style. But then, he was serious about it.

'The Truth of Masks'

'The Truth of Masks' is an essay, in every sense of the term, on the importance of costume to drama, and in particular to the plays of Shakespeare. There is a one-to-one correspondence between the thought conveyed by a scene and the costumes worn by the actors. While instances *Timon of Athens, Macbeth, The Merchant of Venice, Romeo and Juliet,* and so on. He points out Shakespeare's great attention to detail in costume. (It was a paradigm Wilde was to follow in his own plays.) Wilde is arguing for a kind of faithfulness to Shakespeare's intentions: 'Perfect accuracy of detail, for the sake of perfect illusion, is necessary for us.' But there is a greater truth that is observed. 'Truth is independent of facts always, inventing or selecting them at pleasure.' He is not advocating attention to detail of costume over the meaning of the play, but instead to the way it contributes to that meaning.

His closing remarks are typical in that he appears to disown what he is saying – it is an attitude, which is 'everything'. How much of this he meant is challengeable. His references to Plato's theory of forms and Hegel indicate consistency of a kind, or a persistence of an intellectual craving. He wanted to touch on great things. He has not yet found the vehicle suited both to his aims and methods.

'The Soul of Man under Socialism'

This essay was published in the *Fortnightly Review* in 1891, prior to both *Dorian Gray* and *Intentions*. It stands apart from either, in that it ventures into political thought. The essay was inspired by listening to a lecture on socialism, but is not a copy. It is a work of synthesis, bringing together Wilde's theories of art, art criticism, morals, and places them in society, and in so doing it is apparent that society has to change. Amongst other things, it is his response to Arnold's *Culture and Anarchy*. 'The Soul of Man' uses key concepts from Arnold – Hellenism, which is the finer aspect of being (versus Hebraism, which puts doing above being) – Philistinism – the middle classes whom Arnold thought enemies of enlightenment, preferring the 'machinery of business, chapels, tea-meetings' that is worthy perhaps, but dull. The aristocracy, it is interesting to observe, were thought by Arnold to be 'barbarians' interested only in field sports and sports of all kinds. *Culture and Anarchy* was written a generation before 'The Soul of Man', and whilst Wilde was heavily influenced by Arnold, he moves the debate as it were not much further on, but to a different plane of existence. If there is any keynote to Wilde's work – of actually broader interest than *Dorian Gray* – then this essay provides a succinct vision of the meaning of his work. *The Importance of Being Earnest* is explicable using this essay. It contains the themes of all of his work – except one, which is dealt with in the essay 'The Portrait of Mr W.H.', and that is same-sex desire and love.

Wilde opens his 'The Soul of Man' with an attack on conventional morality. Socialism would first 'relieve us of the sordid necessity of living for others'. This is quite unexpected, intended to provoke, and demand an explanation, which is quickly forthcoming. It is easy to sympathise with the plight of the poor and indulge in acts of charity. But these acts are part of the problem: it creates what we nowadays call dependency. 'Charity creates a multitude of sins.' It is primarily the institutions of society that are at fault since

> It is immoral to use private property in order to alleviate the horrible evils that result from the institution of private property. It is both immoral and unfair.

He sees socialism as dealing with this issue. He differs from other socialists in that he sees socialism's function not to be an end in itself but to enable a new kind of individualism.

Cooperation rather than competition will 'restore society to its proper condition of a thoroughly healthy organism'. Socialism is caveated, it requires individualism if the promise of a healthy society is to be realised, and he warns against governments exercising an 'Industrial Tyranny' which would make conditions worse than now. He returns to the attack on charity and property, which result in the degradation of so many: disobedience really is required as a rational response to the conditions of life of multitudes of people. The role of agitators is exemplary, because the crushing nature of poverty makes men unable to act for themselves. Hence slavery is abolished, not by the slaves but by the action of others who agitate against it. In wanting the progress that might be offered by socialism he does not want to universalise the factory system:

> It is to be regretted that a portion of our community should be practically in slavery, but to propose to solve the problem by enslaving the entire community is childish.

The solution is to be found by voluntary association: this is an anarchist and humanitarian position. Individualism has been harmed by the idea of private property 'by confusing a man with what he possesses ... The true perfection of man lies not in what man has but in what man is.' He envisages that 'Nobody will waste his life in accumulating things ... One will live. To live is the rarest thing in the world.'

Wilde's interpretation of Christ is drawn into the debate:

> What Jesus meant was this. He said to man, 'You have a wonderful personality. Develop it. Be yourself. Don't imagine that your perfection lies in accumulating or possessing external things. Your affection is inside of you. If only you could realise that, you would not want to be rich. Ordinary riches can be stolen from a man. Real riches cannot. In the treasury-house of your soul, there are infinitely precious things, that may not be taken from you ... Personal property hinders Individualism at every step.'

This is not the Christ of the pulpit, then – or indeed now.

Wilde sees the institution of property to be the major distortion of society, not only the cause of most crime, but of fracturing the relations of men and women, which ought to be those of love uncluttered by considerations of wealth. Freedom from the restraints of a property-driven society would bring about fundamental change.

Wilde addresses also the issue of the individual and the law. This provides the intellectual framework for his praise of Wainewright in 'Pen Pencil and Poison'. The essence of the argument is that to get the institutions of society to be right, transgressions will disappear. So many of these result from poverty or fear of it, that once need is removed, so the crimes that flow from need disappear. That this is not a complete argument is evident, but it contains an important point of view. Wilde believed that mankind would be naturally virtuous: all that is needed is freedom and trust in the essential nature of man. Odd though that view may seem, the fact of the matter is that the upholding of law depends on it. Finally no law is sustainable if people do not believe it is just and good. It is a re-working of the Socratic theme that true knowledge of virtue means that transgression is impossible.

The role of art in society is pivotal because it is through art that we see the most intense form of individualism. To the objection that art and art appreciation is elitist, he replies that historically that is true: he had in mind the slave-owning Greeks; but that was because society had not evolved. Nevertheless, society would evolve: his belief in Herbert Spencer's evolutionary philosophy – a contemporary fashion of thought is evident. Censorship is abhorrent partly because it suppresses individual expression but mainly because it is destructive. It is evident in science and philosophy that censorship would destroy the activity itself, and so it is with art. The public should endeavour to understand art, not art stoop to the level of the public. He considers the state of the arts in England, where poetry escapes the censorship, because no one reads it, novels are 'badly written' and plays 'silly and vulgar'. The only plays that escape this mediocrity are 'burlesques' and 'farcical' comedies: 'Delightful work may be produced under burlesque and farcical conditions, and in work of this kind the artist in England is allowed very great freedom.' He might well have had the work of W.S. Gilbert in mind. It was advice that he followed, and in seeking to entertain he sought also to subvert and educate, through wit and humour.

He considers the arts and art criticism in great detail. It is the actual point of departure for his philosophy. He dilates at length on the evils of 'Public Opinion' which endeavours to dictate to the artist what should be done. He is savage on the role of journalists and journalism, which have the effect of nullifying art altogether by marshalling prejudices. If anyone approaches a work of art with pre-conceived ideas 'he cannot receive any artistic impression from it at all'. The direction of travel is clear: authority has no role over the artist nor in art, and when it does, it is destructive of the artefact. Art requires individualism, and individualism means the disappearance of authority so that the individual is free to create art. Society will evolve towards this individualism. But this is not an argument for selfishness: individualism is living as one would wish to live, selfishness is asking 'others to live as one wishes to live'. Wilde has no real prescriptions for how people will live in this socialistic society, beyond saying that machines will do the dulling work. The state's role is to manage the distribution of goods, food, shelter and so on.

Finally, he invokes his idea of Christ of the man who abandons or resists 'society absolutely': Christ as the exemplification of the Individualist. Society will evolve to a higher state, in time where such individualism becomes universal. His response to Arnold is poignant: 'Over the portals of the Ancient world is written the words "Know Thyself" and over the portals of the Modern World "Be Thyself". This is the new definition of Hellenism and moves away from Arnold's 'Hebraism'.

'The Portrait of Mr. W.H.'

'The Portrait of Mr. W.H.' is intended as a serious and sustained piece of literary criticism, written from the standpoint of acceptance of Shakespeare's evident homoerotic desires. This essay appeared in a shortened form in *Blackwood's Magazine* in 1889, the fuller version being published in 1920 in America and subsequently in the 1966 Collins Classics edition (and the 1994 edition). The fuller version is considered here. Wilde was very fond of this essay, trying on a number of occasions to get it republished. If *The Canterville Ghost* in effect showed Wilde burying his heterosexual desires, this essay by contrast shows him exulting, through literary history and criticism, in homosexual love and eroticism. It is written as a justification of his feelings. It fantasises about the objects of his desires. Whilst Wilde has been shown to be right about one of the objects of Shakespeare's love (a man) in a large number of the sonnets, the strength of his case is weakened by reference to the actor Willie Hughes. The focus of attention moves from the nature of the desire with its attendant anguish and pleasure, which makes Shakespeare's *Sonnets* so outstanding as literature, to the supposed particular Mr W.H. The theory breaks down at this point, however clever it may be. 'The Portrait of Mr W.H.' is a story, a dialogue and a melodrama, involving the suicide of one character, known only by repute (Cyril Graham) in pursuit of the Willie Hughes theory and the supposed suicide of one of the main characters – Erskine. This is combined with an analysis of the *Sonnets*. The dialogue shows Wilde's ability to construct theory, his ability to range arguments in support of a theory: we would say to conduct a 'thought experiment'. Typically, the essay is intended to work simultaneously on two different levels: those of literary criticism and psychological realism. In this case this means the nature of Shakespeare's and Wilde's sexuality influencing a work of art. As often happens with Wilde, it is none of these things which really work: for example do we really accept that a man committed suicide for a theory? He pointed to, but did not undertake an exegesis of Shakespeare's *Sonnets*. This is a wasted opportunity. On the issue of sexuality, we should come to the point: why should we really care about Wilde's sexuality? Shakespeare's is interesting simply because of the *Sonnets*. Wilde's poetry does not reach that level. A case could be made for *The Picture of Dorian Gray*. Wilde becomes interesting actually because of his self-reflection and then philosophising. He recognised the nature of desire (his) and its objects and then justifies those desires with reference to historical figures. This argument does not work as he intended. Michaelangelo, Montaigne and so on are justly remembered for their work, which suggests that their affections are irrelevant, which is not what Wilde wants to argue. It should be noted that some of the figures he mentions were same-sex lovers, and some were not – they were friends. Conflating the two is deceptive. Humanly, this really is a plea to suspend judgement, which nowadays can be easily granted. The force of his argument is, as so often, tangential: he finally reaches a reconciliation of his feelings, his sense of morals and his intellect by addressing the nature of the mind and in particular, the role of art and the mind.

5

The Stories

WILDE'S TYPICAL MODE OF CONVERSATION IN company was to command the dinner table using a story, or a fable or parable if you will, both to enchant and to illustrate his ideas. Richard Ellmann's biography gives the text of a story, 'The Early Church' placed in Imperial Rome. The protagonists are members of the patrician class. The woman converts to Christianity. To win her love the man converts to Christianity although he is not a believer. In an emperor's persecution of the Christians they are arrested and threatened with being thrown to the lions unless they renounce their beliefs. Terrified, the woman then doubts her beliefs, but does not want her lover to despise her. The man, who is not a believer, likewise does not want her to despise him if he renounces his publicly affirmed faith. As a result both go to their deaths. Hesketh

Pearson's biography relates Wilde recounting the tale to Bernard Shaw of a young inventor who attracts the attention of millionaires for his innovation but, due to an excess of enthusiasm, oversells it and so loses their interest. Wilde thought that the story with its humanising aspect could both delight and provoke people into thought as well as empathising with the theme. Some of these stories – especially those he told his children – are captured in publications. Taken collectively, they are the real spiritual story of Wilde, the writer.

His mind was full of curiosity about his own and thus other people's dilemmas as well as curiosity about the world in the widest sense of that term. He needed to understand the world. In order to reach that understanding it followed that he needed to challenge conventional wisdom – 'the verities'. Narration provided the opportunity to play with ideas and to test them out. Rather like Dickens, whose serialisations provoked feedback from his readers which then went back into his storytelling, the dinner table or children's reaction told Wilde what would, most likely, work. Most of his stories are charming and are still readable. They show a tenderness of mind which is visible in his poetry and a broader perspective on life than his essays published under the title of *Intentions*.

The Canterville Ghost was published in 1887 in the journal *Tribune*. The subtitle, 'A Hylo-Idealistic Romance', that is a tale of conflict of ideas between the material and the spiritual, which indeed it is. And it is also comic, and with so much of Wilde's work it has a number of layers. These layers may be defined as the story itself as a narrative, what it symbolises – which might be a work of imagination by the reader – and what it means for Wilde's development.

The tale is one of an American family headed by a minister of religion, one Hiram B. Otis, and his family settling into Canterville Chase, a house locally renowned for being haunted (placed in Bexley Moor – current-day Bexleyheath, a suburb of London). The family do not take the idea of a ghost seriously at all even though they are formally religious. They expunge ghostly traces – a blood stain – with chemicals. The stain is constantly refreshed by the ghost who is unsettled, even haunted, by the materialism of this family. The ghost, hounded and threatened as it were by redundancy, is able to appeal to the daughter's kinder sensibilities with his story of unrequited love. Finally, the ghost is laid to rest in an elaborate ceremony. Seemingly at one stage in the tale spirituality is routed, but in the end it triumphs. This is the opposite of experience of the modern age. At the same time, Wilde is also laying to rest one kind of love: his heterosexual passion, whilst needing a sympathetic woman (or wisdom) to ensure its transition. The style and content of the story – light-hearted, down to earth yet sentimental and with paradox at its heart, represent a strategy and delivery that is Wildean. It is also one where the mask he habitually wears, slips. The tale works at all levels, and is still fun to read.

1887 saw the publication of more short stories: evidence of creative momentum that gathers pace until Wilde's trials in the mid-1890s. These stories have a certain charm, for example 'The Sphinx Without a Secret', first published in 1887, is of some minor interest: it explores the idea of the importance of privacy and trust in loving relationships. 'The Model Millionaire' might be best described as a confection – which explores the idea that an act of disinterested generosity is handsomely rewarded – which shows Wilde to be sentimental – the opposite let's say of the English saying that 'a good turn never goes unpunished'. But it is 'Lord Arthur Savile's Crime' that merits close attention.

'Lord Arthur Savile's Crime'

This short story is Wilde at his best. He is playing with the philosophical ideas of free will, determinism, fulfilment of prophecy and fatalism. It also finishes on a happy note. Wilde is always more at ease with ending on a note of optimism.

Lord Arthur Savile attends a society party where a cheiromantist, Mr Podgers, is the attraction. Podgers foretells from reading Savile's palm that Savile will commit the crime of murder. Savile becomes obsessed and horrified by this prediction. But it is one which he will have to live out. He resolves to commit a murder: this is the only way to regain his freedom, and to rid himself of the burden of necessity, so to speak. He makes vain attempts to murder people, but fails. Haunted, he prowls despairingly at midnight along the Thames Embankment. And then opportunity! There is Podgers – he seizes him 'by the legs' and throws him into the River Thames. All that remains after the splash is ' ... a tall hat, pirouetting in an eddy of moonlit water'. Savile gets away with his crime and is happy to live with himself. He marries happily at the close of the tale. It is a wish fulfilment – doing 'wrong' because it is necessary – and being able to carry on living happily in 'society' – that is with the social acceptance that is so necessary. Wilde was fascinated by transgression and his belief that it flowed from an individual's essential nature. Society might discover the crime; recognise it by punishing the individual, but ideally neither of these.

Wilde's art and plotting follow a pattern that is familiar: a serious theme; light witty dialogue; a life-changing drama; aesthetics and poetry, and a resolution that is happy. There is a certainty, but a lightness of touch, an originality of phrasing that is charming. The writer is in control of his subject matter, and the tale is indicative both of how Wilde's art began and how it will develop. There are a number of features of the tale that illustrate this point.

One is the dialogue, for example, of the aristocratic and well-to-do party-goers where Podgers gives his palm reading, which prefigures that of the comedies, with exchanges about marriage, losing distant relatives, the role of young men in society, etc.

Another is the contrast of the style with the subject matter – it steers somehow away from the darker note that *The Picture of Dorian Gray* strikes. Though the emotional turmoil that Savile experiences approaches Gray's horrors, it is lightened by the way the story is told. It prefigures, in parts *The Importance of Being Earnest* in its persiflage.

It contains passages of fluid, poetic writing, some of which is worth quoting – where Savile is out at night on the Embankment of the Thames:

> … The moon peered through a mane of tawny clouds, as if it were a lion's eye, and innumerable stars spangled the hollow vault, like gold dust powdered on a purple dome. Now and then a barge swung out into the turbid stream, and floated away with the tide, and railway signals changed from green to scarlet as the trains ran shrieking across the bridge. After some time, twelve o' clock boomed from the tall tower at Westminster, and at each stroke of the sonorous bell the night seemed to tremble. Then the railway lights went out, one solitary lamp left gleaming like a large ruby on a giant mast, and the roar of the city became fainter. (Chapter 5)

There are echoes of Wilde's poems in this:

Impressions
La Mer

A white mist drifts across the shrouds,
A wild moon in this wintry sky
Gleams like an angry lion's eye
Out of a mane of tawny clouds ...

This is Wilde, quoting himself (which he habitually did) reusing phrases intelligently, to symbolise Savile's isolation.

Stories for children

These are stories that Wilde told to his children and subsequently collected into two publications: *The Happy Prince & Other Tales* (1888) dedicated to Carlos Blacker and *A House of Pomegranates* (1891) which he dedicated to his wife. There is sufficient evidence to suggest that she collaborated in some of these stories.

The stories are essentially fables or moral tales designed to enchant, amuse and educate the audience – which seems to be equally comprised of adults as well as children. Some carefully worded asides set out to engage with this varied audience:

> ... So cold was it that even the animals and the birds did not know what to make of it.
> 'Ugh!' snarled the Wolf, as he limped through the brushwood with his tail between his legs, 'this is perfectly monstrous weather. Why doesn't the government look to it?'
>
> ('The Star Child')

Wilde's subject matter is often difficult, which is reflected in the conflict of style and content. He could tell a tale with a single coherent theme in a straightforward way – and generally these stories are the most successful, but others seem to be less under his control and are overburdened in their telling. The better told and more interesting tales are rewarding.

'The Happy Prince'

This story is one of sacrifice to help others in need. The statue of the Prince – the so-called 'Happy Prince' who had led a life of pleasure without regard for others (but can that be called happy?) – gives up his gold leaf and jewels in his rather all-too-material afterlife, to help the poor with the aid of a swallow. Both the swallow and the statue are sacrificed in this endeavour – and are forgotten on earth. Recognition and reward come from God. The story enchants through repetition of acts of kindness in varying forms until the inevitable end: and so the child asks – what happens then?

'The Birthday of the Infanta'

The Infanta – the royal princess of Spain – who is the centre of attention all of her young life and is as a consequence selfish, has entertainments laid on for her birthday. Amongst these is a dance given by a Dwarf, who has been kept from human contact. She finds the dance funny –

because it is so grotesque. She asks for the Dwarf to perform for her again. The Dwarf believes that she cares for him and he falls in love with her. He searches vainly for her round the palace and in so doing sees himself in the mirror for the first time. There he sees himself as he actually is, hunchbacked and in his own eyes grotesque. The realisation is that he is seen only as a freak. This breaks his heart and he dies. The Infanta is merely frustrated by this and says: 'For the future let those who come to play with me have no hearts.' This is a sustained fantasy complete with flowers, sundials all conversing with one another, displaying human foibles. All nature and human nature are one, and all are in conversation with one another making a social commentary. Some creatures are exempt from this moral obloquy:

> … But somehow the Birds liked him. They had seen him often in the forest, dancing about like an elf after the eddying leaves, or crouched up in the hollow of some old oak tree, sharing his nuts with the squirrels. They did not mind his being ugly, a bit.

The burden of the story is that there is no human redeeming force. Social conventions do not give redemption: this comes from a wider 'force' of Nature or God. Wilde is unequivocal about the need for redemption, love and forgiveness, if not about the agency that provides it.

'The Selfish Giant'

Redemption comes for the Selfish Giant who excludes children from his beautiful garden. The garden responds by becoming immersed in a perpetual winter where nothing grows and the sun does not shine. This changes when the children find their way back in through a hole in the wall round the Giant's garden. The Giant realises how selfish he has been – and how delightful it is to give joy to others. A small distressed child is helped into a tree by the Giant. The Giant tears down the wall to enable children to play. Thereafter the garden thrives. The little boy does not return until the end of the Giant's life – and when he does he has wounds ' … the wounds of love'. The child symbolises Christ who is the Giant's redeemer.

This story has echoes: C.S. Lewis uses the theme of a frozen, evil world in his Narnia stories.

'The Remarkable Rocket'

In Wilde's own examination of his work and its impact, fear of failure cannot have been far away. The Remarkable Rocket has a very high opinion of himself: he is superior to all the other fireworks that are due to be let off in celebration of the King's son's wedding. (Wilde's declaration at New York Customs: 'I have nothing to declare except my genius').

The Remarkable Rocket's view is quite different from all the other fireworks:

... how fortunate it is for the King's son, ... that he is to be married on the very day on which I am to be let off!

His whole view is egocentric – imagining that he has friendship with the Prince – and expressing anxiety over imagined disasters the Prince and his bride might have to endure, finally parading his sensitivity to the point where he bursts into real tears. As a result the Rocket does not go off. He is discovered later by two small boys who think he is merely an old stick – and put him on to a fire that they are building. He finally does ignite and goes up into the air – but no one sees him. The Rocket's last words are: 'I knew I should create a great sensation ... '

The story, its manner of telling, the use of witty dialogue combined with its brevity make it psychologically astute and readable. It summarises Wilde's fears about his actual achievement as a writer contrasted with his perception of his gifts of learning and creativity.

What distinguishes these children's stories from others are the tensions between ideas: the conflict between the 'will' and the 'world': what we might want and what there is, as well as between what is considered socially to be acceptable and what on the other hand is 'good'.

Poems in Prose

It seems sensible to group Wilde's prose poems under the heading of stories or fables. Influenced by Baudelaire, he wrote prose poems – an awkward category – being neither verse nor quite lengthy enough to rank as short stories. They are essentially plot summaries that might have been worked up into stories. Unlike Baudelaire's prose poems, Wilde's are fables or parables rather than the imagery, resonance of words or ideas that we would associate with poetry. They are all thought experiments put into a tale to illustrate a point.

Of these, the most effective prose poem is 'The Disciple', which deconstructs discipleship into narcissism: ' … I loved Narcissus because, as he lay on my banks and looked down at me, in the mirror of his eyes I saw ever my own beauty mirrored.'

It is a challenge to the conventional meaning of disci-pleship. Apart from 'The Disciple' the prose poem 'The Doer of Good' postulates a Christ-like figure who cures people of their maladies only to find them leading lives of lust and indolence: their excuse is simply – this what they do: it is in their nature and there are no other possibilities. This is the kind of 'runs on rails' fatalism that is a constant theme in Wilde's work.

Most of the prose poems are essays in religion, a play upon the reality of human existence and necessities versus the religious view of man as conveyed in New Testament accounts. Generally the received view of religion comes off worst. In the final poem 'The Teacher of Wisdom', knowledge of God which the Hermit has, is given away –

but is replaced by the love of God. This is as close to mysticism, as conventionally understood, that Wilde gets.

Wilde was to return to biblical and religious themes in his minor plays and oral stories. He endeavours to raise these themes into debate and to move into new intellectual (and emotional) territory. Of these the most complete play is *Salomé*.

6

The Picture of Dorian Gray

THERE IS A DESIRE AMONGST MANY people to see *The Picture of Dorian Gray* as predominantly, if not exclusively, a novel concerning homoeroticism, giving expression to homoerotic feelings, tending to celebrate them. The novel is neither that simple nor as whole-hearted as might be supposed. It is tentative and ambiguous. *Dorian Gray* is not *Teleny*. *Teleny* is an underground *samizdat* novel in circulation at that time – attributed to Wilde and very possibly the work also of other hands. It is a tale of passion, of love between two young men, for *cognoscenti* only. It makes it as clear as may be how someone falls for someone else. The fact that this form of love is forbidden since it is love between two men, is in a sense circumstantial. It wears the character of all forbidden love, whether across class boundaries, allegiances or any other barrier to the expression of love and passion. By contrast, *Dorian Gray* is a novel about the self – its window on the world is through the development of the self (or 'soul').

Dorian Gray echoes Robert Louis Stevenson's *Dr Jekyll and Mr Hyde* story. It is a Gothic novel – which demands the willing and complete suspension of disbelief to get off the ground. In *Dorian Gray* the public persona is everlastingly young and the 'real' and thus the private person (the picture locked away in an attic) has become corrupted by sin and time. The story is also Faustian: it explores the extreme cultivation of the intellect and the senses which results in feelings of such power that it must lead to destruction. The pact made by Faust with the Devil that gives rise to illusory power and pleasures that are finally hollow, is paralleled in Wilde's book by a whim being mysteriously granted to retain the outward appearance of youth. There is a price to be paid: the picture becomes one of a man disfigured (by evil) and it cannot be shown to the public.

By contrast again, the prose of *Teleny* is straightforward: it has none of the characteristics of the patchwork of epigram and elaborate prose that characterises *Dorian Gray. Teleny* has an urgency which is born of a reality that has momentum within it. Dorian's demise in *Dorian Gray* is melodramatic and contrived. The form Wilde's prose takes is similar to that of his poetry: the more elaborate and self-consciously styled, the less there is in strength of subject matter.

The Picture of Dorian Gray was first published in a

serialised form in *Lippincott's Magazine*. It created a critical storm, attracting largely hostile comment based on its perceived decadence – true; plagiarism – an easy target; and its homoeroticism. The book version is a re-edit of the serialisation and adds a Preface. This Preface, couched in epigrammatic Nietzchean-seeming phrases, sees Wilde coming out of his corner, fighting. It defiantly expresses this aesthetic credo in a way that is calculated to arouse passion. It is really a separate work from *Dorian Gray*. On analysis, though, its simplifications are exaggerations, not really that persuasive, and are quite defensive: ' … That is all.' It lacks the maturity and subtlety of 'The Critic as Artist'. The Preface is quotable, but that is to be expected. It is intended to guide the humble reader away from what is rather obvious – that the book is read easily as a moral tale, showing the psychological consequences of a narcissistic, hedonistic and loveless life.

Even so, taken at face value, the Preface misleads in two ways. In respect of style, the Preface's condensed concise style is at odds with the long-paced prose inspired by J.K. Huysmans' *À Rebours* (translated as *Against Nature* or *Against the Grain*) published in 1884. *À Rebours* is the definitive decadent work, moving French as well as literature in Engish away from Zola's realism and inaugurating a style of literature that was to reach its final fruition in France with Proust's *À La Recherche du Temps Perdu*.

The style of *Dorian Gray* is a mixture of contrasting

styles, periods of purple prose contrasted with dialogue that is epigrammatic but stagey, artificial and awkward – as if the characters never really say what they mean. Some of the sharper utterances find their way subsequently into *Lady Windermere's Fan*. It sits oddly in the descriptive, highly coloured prose that surrounds it. The Preface states that the only way of evaluating *Dorian Gray* is as a work of art. That is a very high demand, and if acceded to, means that the book is wanting. As a work of art, it is a melodrama, and this from a man who said 'One must have a heart of stone to read the death of Little Nell without laughing.' The circumstances of the death of Sibyl Vane, to take one example, lack conviction, except at the level that Gray is not really interested in her or women at all. That she commits suicide as a result of the engagement being broken off – and that because of a poor stage performance – is unlikely. In any socio-economic reality recognisable to Victorians, Sibyl's mother would have demanded and received a financial settlement. Sibyl has to go, and this has to be a 'sin', and, as such, is necessary for the plot.

To repeat, the work is moral. Gray is consumed by his quest for pleasurable sensations that prove empty. He cannot be satisfied. He struggles to fight off the *ennui* of an existence that is validated only by conspicuous consumption, luxury and a self-consciously decadent taste in art. In celebrating the senses, the absence of a deeper meaning to life makes the whole enterprise unrewarding, and this in turn makes Gray more savage and cruel.

The novel is not 'just' about same-sex attraction, its aim is wider than that. It is about freedom of thought to explore life – which is the function of art. Significantly, the starting point is the work of art: Dorian Gray's picture. The work of art through which reality is interpreted actually changes: it is a human body that does not. This is an inversion of what art is. This is Wilde testing his ideas about the centrality of art to our knowledge of the world. Dorian the man is a work of art and the embodiment of the idea of beauty – which is also the idea of the Dandy. The reality that this man creates – one of ransacking ideas and art forms to cultivate a personality which in turn exploits the people with whom he comes into contact – is, as J.A. Symonds (a sympathetic critic) said, 'unwholesome'. Order is restored on Dorian's death – the man is aged and the painting unchanged.

Attraction of men for men is not fully explored but only hinted at, in the sense that Walt Whitman expressed as 'comradeship'. Lord Henry Wotton is too detached as an observer, too much the mentor, and Gray too incomplete as a man for there to be a credible relationship of real depth. Same-sex love and desire turn into a mess of pottage. Relationships are referred to but not explored, and they end disastrously for the victims, but not Gray. Commercial sex is available in low-life conditions – which is its appeal also (Wilde refers in his letters to 'feasting with Panthers'), but it does not satisfy. There is no love, there is sin and self-destruction. This could be read as a tragedy of a wasted life seeking sensation only and not love: a life that has seemingly everything and puts it to no use. Gray's 'code' of behaviour is the self-serving morality of greed and lust. It is de-humanising. Seeking more, leads to finding less: and is thus a critique of purposeless materialism.

But the book does work in another sense. There being no other way that would be acceptable at the time, it obliquely offers a critique of a society that represses, pointlessly, the expression of same-sex love. This repression leads to displacement, desolation and destructive despair. *Dorian Gray* is a clarion call to the sexual underdog: and for those who know what is meant this is very important. H.H. Munro ('Saki') quotes from *Dorian Gray* in his *Rise of the Russian Empire* (1900), p. 251: 'A brilliant writer, drawing his materials from the history of mediaeval Italy both before and after the Renaissance, … has pictured the awful and beautiful forms of those whom vice and blood and weariness had made monstrous or mad … ' He knew what Wilde meant and liked that, as did a fellow prisoner of Wilde's at Reading Gaol. Those in the know, read *Dorian Gray*. They are typified also by Proust (*À La Recherche du Temps Perdu*) as those pale youths hanging about railway stations, hoping for an encounter with another male, being denied all other modes of more civilised sexual expression. If the book is talking coherently, this is the work at its most coherent. For social reasons same-sex relationships are forced into sexual intrigue and conquest, which have their moments, but open love is denied them. Many critics, sensing the drift of Wilde's sign language, hated it, not for aesthetic reasons, but because they disliked that form of sexual expression. Where the Preface says: 'No artist is ever morbid. The artist can express everything' Wilde is replying in part to those critics, but, more significantly, commenting on Aristotle. Wilde's thought was significantly influenced by Aristotle. Unlike Socrates and Plato, Aristotle was hetero-sexual, and he held (*Nicomachean Ethics*) that same-sex expression is morbid. Wilde, through the ages, must reply.

Dorian Gray depicts obliquely rather than directly the predicament of an unaccepted sexuality. Sexuality does not have to be criminalised to be despised. Gray leads a double life. He is a gentleman of high society, but leads his truer life, where he is able to express his nature, away from his peer group: in the 'low' life where, paradoxically, he could also feel 'superior'. Wilde's ambiguity is expressed in the concept of 'sin'. This particular 'sin' was both exciting, and necessary, but it was still wrongdoing. At the heart of this dilemma is the question of love, coupled or uncoupled with desire: a loveless life is not worth having.

Dorian Gray is a vision of a life. In this vision, each man is alone in his moral dilemma, isolated in his despairing reflections, treading carefully in a world that is going to persecute the unwary. A succession of 'friends' or 'lovers' do not amount to the same as the friend described by

Montaigne in his essay 'On Friendship'. Dorian's picture records everything and cannot be hidden. It is a parable, like others of Wilde's: moral at its heart.

Artistically, *Dorian Gray* ranks with both Wilde's best and worst. It is not actually, as one critic says, 'a novelette', but it could be seen that way. The plot can be mawkish and melodramatic. The theme can be seen as confusing and self-contradictory. The truth is that Wilde's methodology – using pre-existing models and synthesising them – is not under control. A better account of decadence is given in *À Rebours* by J.K. Huysmans; and the angst of forbidden, unrequited same-sex passion better explored in Thomas Mann's *Death in Venice*. The book is a monodrama of the soul like these others. But, unlike them, the struggle of a man coming to self-knowledge and then *being* himself, is depicted through the poses and the multiplicity of personalities – Wotton, Hallward and Gray.

It is also a critical survey of the cultural landscape of an age. As a lexicon of poetry, prose and art the reader is pointed to works that are in themselves significant, and which repay investigation. Wilde thought of himself as 'standing in a symbolic relationship' to his age, and in this sense *Dorian Gray* backs up that claim. It is also a pioneering novel, acknowledging the claims of same-sex attraction. Its limitations are those of narcissism. It is also, on a more elevated plane, a view of what self-development should be in the modern age: that age is not so dissimilar from our own. It is also a kind of textbook surveying and defining the idea of decadence; should a reader wish to imbibe the ideas and sensations of decadence – this is a kind of 'Lonely Planet' guide to that. Where does it lead? The question was postulated by critics of *À Rebours*, the work which above others influenced the writing of *Dorian Gray*. In the case of Huysmans it leads either to despair, suicide or to refuge in religion. In this work, it leads to self-destruction. Wilde explored the nature of love for others, self-love and its relation to lust more fully in his dramas.

Proust said of his own work *À La Recherche du Temps Perdu* that it was a work in part about pederasty. If so, André Gide thought that the book showed pederasty in the poorest possible light – love is confined to the female figures whilst Jupien and the Baron de Charlus are shown as depraved or pathetic. The panorama of *À La Recherche* and its exploration of the kinds of love, society and the nature of time in a comic, satirical way, can be contrasted with *Dorian Gray*, which has a narrower focus: more or less completely on the self and its self-conscious development. The passion at the centre of the work is narcissism. The tone of the book is such that it does not analyse or poke fun at itself or the society it represents. Like R.L. Stevenson's *Dr Jekyll and Mr Hyde*, the novel starts off with the great self-confidence of the central idea – the transformation of a soul, the bravado of youth – only to see this confidence melt as the limitations of the idea are made to unfold by events.

Dorian Gray is like many of Wilde's works: an extended thought experiment. It is the test bed of ideas. Wilde's early endorsement of the cult of beauty and hedonism is projected into this book. Its limitations he progressively realised elsewhere, in his essays, for example 'The Soul of Man under Socialism', and in the stories he wrote for his children 'The Happy Prince' and 'The Birthday of the Infanta'. Wilde wanted to be able to say *anything* – there is no immoral thought: 'There is no such thing as a moral or an immoral book.' He was not writing pornography, either.

Love and Desire

The characters around Dorian Gray are united in their passion for him: this is not so much love as desire. Basil Hallward's desire is expressed in terms of physical beauty and overcoming his fear of absorption by Gray through portraiture. Gray's retaliation is to deny him possession of the portrait.

Lord Henry Wotton's seduction of Gray – and Hallward tries to keep Gray away from Wotton the seducer – is competitive with Hallward's desire for possession and is mediated through language – dialogue: books, ideas and provocative, antinomian thought. Wotton is the formative influence. Wotton's analysis of society, his insouciance, neglect of his wife and his indifference to her leaving him show a detachment that in the hands of Gray become self-serving and cruel. It becomes apparent that the disciple

Gray outruns the master. Self-determination and, in particular, the notion of the individual without the claims of others on the personality leads to isolation and paranoia.

Time and Decay

Where time is dealt with it is on the level of it being the enemy of physical beauty: the passage of time equates to the accretion of sins, which are recorded on the portrait which must be hidden from view. Fear of discovery of sins is symbolised by ugliness in the portrait. Why should such a self-confident being fear the judgement of society? The loss of physical beauty is the crime: despised, not being lusted after, is the failing. The portrait *is* the reality, the body is the surface. This becomes inverted: the body is made to be timeless. Dorian's portrait is the inversion of portraiture – which catches a person at a point in time whilst the person changes and drifts away from the picture. The picture becomes the mirror of the soul.

Self-development and Power: Faust

It is a very modern concept that an individual can have, if only he wills it, power over his life. There is talk in our era of scripting a person's life – and this is not meant in an ironic way. *Dorian Gray* is an essay in this vein: Gray cultivates his learning; it is directed towards decadent and recherché authors and artists. He explores Darwin and science: his learning is wide and deep where he chooses it to be. He has beauty, social standing, brains and wealth. What could possibly go wrong?

The role of Lord Henry Wotton becomes rather like that of Mephistopheles in Marlowe's *Dr Faustus*. As with Mephistopheles, Wotton happens to pass by: he is the demon seducer of a virgin soul. He conquers Gray with his philosophy, which is an extreme kind of hedonism that chases the pleasures whilst acknowledging the fleeting moment. In the sense that the legend of Faust is an inversion of the Temptation of Christ in the wilderness, so Wotton, struck by Gray's beauty, must have him – or have a decisive influence over him. This is power actuated by desire: but is not love. And like Faust, Gray succumbs to the prospect of a life which apparently conforms to his will.

Gray is superficially able to direct his life – he has wealth and with it the power over the ordinary circumstances of life – where someone might live, eat, drink, travel – that money gives. The limitations of the individual will are described – this becomes apparent in Gray's interaction with other people. Gray's self-centred nature alienates him from others. He has desire, but it is not love. His greatest sympathy for living things other than himself is for animals. And finally his self-disgust overcomes even his self-love. His corruption is recorded in his portrait, which functions as kind of judgement-day ledger, which he hides from others. Fear of discovery, paranoia about keeping his secret which he cannot hide from himself continually haunts him.

Apparently gifted with all the necessary apparatus of freedom Gray is increasingly confined by his actions: his universe is shrunk by his need to avoid discovery and recrimination.

The Movement of Mind in *Dorian Gray*

The action of the book is set in the social milieu of Britain's leisured classes in the 1890s, who lived on rents, remittances, dividends and so forth and did not have to work for a living. Their days could be filled with the social round: 'society', as it was called; dinner parties, balls and so on. Refinement of intellect, art appreciation, theatre-going, conversation, as well as the more obvious diversions of sports were all possible and in point of fact, ritualised. The main enemy was boredom, which led to overindulgence in vices and worst of all disclosure of them, resulting in scandal and ostracism.

The opening chapters establish male beauty and personality as admired by other men. The discussion initially is conducted via contemplation of Dorian Gray's portrait – Art is, as ever, central to Wilde's thinking. Wilde refines his views and says through one of his alter egos, Lord Henry Wotton that: ' ... every portrait that is painted with feeling is a portrait of the artist, not of the sitter. The sitter is merely the accident, the occasion ... ' Accident is a philosophical term: Wilde's technique is to turn the apparently self-evident upside down. As ever, it is not wholly true nor is it wholly false and it sets the argument going.

Basil Hallward and Wotton have a mutual understanding and susceptibility about male beauty. Wotton has to conquer the youth whereas Basil Hallward is obsessed and is the weaker of the two men. He says of Gray, the beautiful young man, that his ' ... personality was so fascinating that if I allowed it to do so, it would absorb my whole nature, my whole soul, my very art itself.' Wotton seemingly is socially competent, is married as would be expected, but is distanced from the institution: ' ... the one charm of marriage is that it makes a life of deception absolutely necessary for both parties', as well as from his wife:

> 'I never know where my wife is, and my wife never knows what I am doing. When we meet ... we tell each other the most absurd stories with the most serious faces ... '

and

> ' ... when she does find me out, she makes no row at all. I sometimes wish she would, but she merely laughs at me ... '

This level of ironic detachment derives from a lack of sexual interest certainly but artistically also from the difficulty of placing a wife in this mental landscape. Wotton and his wife are friends at best. There is no real insight into her. She leaves Wotton eventually, but this is seen solely through Wotton's speech. There is at least a description of the actress Sybil Vane's feelings. Gray has an infatuation for her that evaporates once she gives a poor acting performance, and as a consequence he then discards her.

It is not until the book is under way that in Chapter 2 Gray actually appears. Wotton has his way in meeting Gray. Gray plays coquettishly to Wotton and there is mutual fascination. This is the occasion for Wilde to spell out his analysis of life: in discussing the influence one person has over another he inverts the obvious relationship – the one having most influence surrenders his personality and no longer thinks 'his natural thoughts, or burns with his natural passions … he becomes an echo of someone else's music, an actor of a part that has not been written for him … '

In order to win over Gray, Wotton sets about astounding him with ideas and paradoxes, whilst praising his looks. His speculations about the soul and the senses are explored in Chapter 10 of this book. It may be asked what place these speculations have in a novel. It makes the book more of a manifesto about art, life and morals.

At the same time, Hallward is becoming besotted with Gray as well as adoring the portrait. Gray himself is a petulant youth and resents the portrait's permanence compared to his own transient beauty. The wish never to age is mysteriously to be granted. Gray *de facto* abandons Hallward and goes off with Wotton. Hallward flings himself on a sofa in despair: it should be noted that characters in this book seem always to be flinging themselves on to sofas. No wonder this is called the leisured class …

Wotton's fascination with Gray grows. In a later chapter, he explores Gray's background. At the same time Wotton's musings are also detached: his obsession is anatomised:

> … To project one's soul into some gracious form, and let it tarry there for a moment; to hear one's own intellectual views echoed back to one with all the added music of passion and youth …

It leaves no doubt about the nature of the desire Wotton has: it is about himself and his wish to make Gray a disciple – possessing him – also that Wotton may get a better view of himself. It is an essay in narcissism. Whatever else it may be, this is not the description of love, but rather of the objectification of a person into an artefact of desire.

Early in the book too, dialogue sharpened and put into the mouths of people Wotton encounters, has an almost separate momentum as if the book is endeavouring to become a play. Wotton tests ideas in conversation with friends and acquaintances. The role of paradox in Wilde's thought is made clear:

> ' … the way of paradoxes is the way of truth. To test Reality we must see it on the tight rope. When the verities become acrobats, we can judge them … '

In Wilde's comedies this sort of strategy makes for amusement and provokes thought. *Dorian Gray*, for all its wit, is not a comedy of any kind and as a result these ideas are darker – sinister, and threatening.

Having embraced the hedonistic, decadent life, the consequences for Gray become clearer: as he commits each 'sin' or transgression, this is recorded in the picture – to the point where it has to be hidden from view and becomes the object of secrecy and paranoia. It leads Gray to murder Hallward to prevent discovery, and in self-loathing objectified in Gray's contemplation of his own portrait, leads to Gray's suicide. The story is one of destruction and dehumanisation.

The pattern of the book is an elaboration of the stages of that journey. It is a fusion of philosophy, an expression of sexual orientation and passion, fear of the loss of beauty, of social influence, of science, and a lexicon of decadent literature and art. This is dangerously close to being a textbook. It is a tale also of supernatural forces – a development of the way that Wilde's *The Canterville Ghost* works. In *Dorian Gray* an unspecified extra-mundane force is the mechanism that drives the plot: the reader is required to accept that a picture reflects the state of Gray's soul, as that state changes.

Dorian Gray is, or represents, a state of mind. In a letter dashed off to a correspondent Wilde says as much:

> Art is useless because its aim is simply to create to create
> a mood ... A work of art is as useless as a flower is useless.
> A flower blossoms for its own joy. We gain a moment of
> joy by looking at it. That is all that is to be said about our
> relations to flowers ...

He distinguishes later in the letter between *essence* and *accident*, a philosophical point. In this respect Wilde might be held to succeed in terms of his own definition of a work of art. All other attributes (accidents) are not of the essence of a work of art. But is the creation of a mood sufficient?

In his *Letters* Wilde refers to *Dorian Gray* as that 'curious jewel' which in a sense it is: it defies the normal categories despite having the usual narrative form of a novel. There is no doubt that it is a serious piece of work. Whatever limitations it has, its purposes and mode of expression were understood by writers and critics as diverse as Pater, Mallarmé and Maeterlinck.

7

Salomé and the Minor Plays

WILDE ASPIRED TO WRITE SERIOUS PLAYS, as his first play *Vera* indicates. For a man who created laughter through his dramas this seems odd. Temperamentally, Wilde was not essentially a tragedian. He would have been aware that tragedy is seen to be the highest form of dramatic art. Interestingly, he thought that *King Lear*, surely one of the greatest tragic plays, is ' … poor life struggling through fog … ' He would have felt that he had the intellectual apparatus for the highest seriousness but in reality, in his hands, the tragic tends toward the melodramatic. Even with this limitation the best of his work in this genre, *Salomé*, has proved to be influential.

Vera; or, The Nihilists
Wilde was drawn to the theatre. He saw it as a natural

development of his art. You may have an audience for table talk, so why not one at a theatre? He learned from Dion Boucicault, whom he met on his tour of the United States, that plays can make fortunes. He wrote *Vera; or, The Nihilists* to capitalise not only on his fame, but on the contemporary and emerging interest in subversive movements in Russia. There is no evidence that Wilde or his audience had much direct acquaintance with Russia, any more than a modern audience would have much direct experience of conflict in Afghanistan – only what the newspapers and various media say. H.H. Munro's book *The Rise of the Russian Empire* published in 1900 was aimed explicitly at addressing this deficiency. The play would have to overcome the obstacles of a lack of knowledge of what political intrigue in a totalitarian regime actually would mean, as well as lack of knowledge of the Russian ethos. It would require dramatic momentum of considerable force to create a credible drama. Shakespeare worked with similar disadvantages but could make a play. *Vera* does not have that impetus. *Vera* played in New York for a short period of time but did not take. The play is not really of intrinsic dramatic or literary interest. However, extrinsically, it is part of Wilde's biography. It is very much a 'prentice work. For example, he padded the play out with Masonic rituals to add to a scene. There are indications that he could animate a play with witty remarks, which makes it more important as a marker in his artistic development than anything else.

It does not reward the effort of exegesis.

The Duchess of Padua

The play's setting is Renaissance Italy. It is a revenge tragedy of the type that flourished in late Elizabethan and Jacobean times and was revived in France in the 19th century by Hugo and Dumas.

The principal character, Guido Ferranti (the original title of the play), is to avenge his father's death at the hands of the Duke of Padua. The story's dramatic tension is raised by Guido falling in love with the Duke's wife Beatrice – a love that is returned. Guido leaves his dagger in the Duke's bedroom to show that he could have killed him. Instead Beatrice kills the Duke with the dagger, which repels Guido. She protects herself by having Guido arrested. He is tried for murder and is due to be executed. She has a change of heart and tries to confess to the murder but is not believed. She drinks poison and visits Guido who in turn kills himself with a dagger. The play itself was probably inspired in part by Hugo, whose success Wilde wished to emulate. Artistically, Wilde is testing his capacity to create and maintain dramatic tension. It would not be too much to suppose that Wilde's model was also Shakespeare. That is the implied invitation. It works well enough, but whether it is Wilde's reputation for wit and comedy that clouds the judgement or there is an irritation with its lines, is at times difficult to tell. The end result is clear enough: it is melodrama rather than tragedy.

A *Florentine Tragedy* and *La Sainte Courtisane*

A *Florentine Tragedy* is incomplete but is tenable as a drama. It is set in Renaissance Italy. The main action comprises a dialogue between two men, one of whom (Simone) is certain that the other (Guido) is having an affair with his wife. There is an engagement between the two characters which is like a bloodlusting animal in pursuit of another. There is a sense in which the outcome is inevitable: Simone is determined to corner his prey. The issue for the main protagonist is how to trap the other in a fight so that it becomes justifiable killing. When the event occurs, the act of killing rekindles the 'love' or rather desire of Simone's wife for her husband. How credible this is depends wholly on the atmosphere created by the play – and at this point this potentially difficult transition becomes viable – disbelief is suspended. This type of inversion is a favourite theme of Wilde's. Sexual desire and obsession lead to unpredictable outcomes. This theme is repeated elsewhere – in *La Sainte Courtisane* as well as in *Salomé*. Wilde is stating what for him is obvious, but others need persuasion through the drama. His ability to achieve this has shifted – this is the effect of writing *Salomé* – whatever may be said about that play it was written when Wilde's creative powers were rising.

La Sainte Courtisane is an even more fragmentary play – the main version of which was lost by Wilde in a cab in Paris after his release from prison. Myrrhina is a wealthy noblewoman who travels to the desert outside Alexandria in Egypt to tempt Honorius, a Christian hermit, into a life of pleasure. The flow of the fragment is that the two characters go in contrary directions – she is persuaded by his abstinence and he by her physical charms. These themes of conflicting ideology, in this case between paganism with its sensuality and Christian ideas of self-denial, are recurring ideas. This play is yet another example. What remains of the play is not worth intense study except possibly as a way of viewing the totality of his dramatic work.

Salomé

Salomé was written originally in French. It was part of Wilde's aim to be recognised in France as well as Britain – no mean enterprise. Significantly, Wilde was inspired by *Hérodias*, one of Flaubert's *Trois Contes* (which deals with the story of John the Baptist) and that in turn by the biblical account. Wilde took the idea and gave it fresh impetus and a new meaning. A cartoon of the time depicts Wilde, with mascara round his eyes, reading Gautier with Flaubert's book beside him together with an English–French dictionary. Wilde was a fluent reader of French and could certainly more than hold his own in conversation in French. Nevertheless he had the text checked by his French writer friend Pierre Louÿs. Wilde agreed with Sarah Bernhardt that she should put on the play in London and act in it. The play was published in France in 1893 and the English translation by Alfred Douglas and corrected by Wilde was published in 1894. It was illustrated by Aubrey Beardsley – one of the avant-garde illustrators of the day. Its reception in France was warm as its reception in Britain was hostile. It was played in France in 1896 whilst he was in prison: it was not played in Britain until after his death.

As Wilde's text does not follow biblical accounts, it creates its own terms of reference, whilst paradoxically depending on Scripture for authority and also to gain the audience's attention. It is saying in effect: here is a creative, plausible interpretation of events. It is a deliberate challenge to received doctrine. Given the temper of the times, and the fact that English law forbade the portrayal of biblical characters in plays, it is unsurprising that the Lord Chamberlain – charged with licensing plays would forbid the production of the play which might be considered in conflict with the *mores* of the day.

Salomé has to be viewed in two ways: the first, the conflict of ideas and passions and the outcomes – that is the plot; and then presentation of these ideas – the quality of the text and drama.

The setting is New Testament times in the court of Herod, ruler of Palestine under the Roman Empire. He has custody of the holy man, Jokanaan – also the form of the name chosen by Flaubert, more usually known as John the Baptist. Herod's step-daughter Salomé, for whom it emerges Herod has an incestuous sexual desire, has in turn a violently strong passion sexually to possess the holy man. Her advances are rejected by Jokanaan, whose vocation overcomes any desire he might have felt. This provides the momentum behind Salomé's revenge: unable to fulfil her desires she will exert power over him. In place of sexual power, power is expressed by causing his death, which she does by displacing the guilt on to another but more susceptible, man: Herod. Herod is depicted as a conflicted, gross figure driven by desires. His wife Herodias (Salomé's mother) despises him and taunts him about his low birth: she is of royal blood. Herodias colludes with Salomé in proposing the dance of the seven veils. This is another working of the revenge theme – in her case vengeance for Jokanaan's denunciation of her marriage to Herod.

Salomé's price for the dance is Jokanaan's head on a platter. Despite his fear of the prophet's holy status Herod's lusts overcome his aversion and he accedes to the request. It is a promise that has to be kept: no alternative will do, even as he promises virtually anything as a substitute. But even he is revolted when Salomé kisses the mouth of the prophet's head on the platter, and so orders Salomé's execution.

The plot of *Salomé* has exercised considerable influence in European culture – Richard Strauss was moved to create his opera *Salomé* as was Antoine Mariotte. Since that time the same theme has influenced the production of films as well as plays.

If the idea has proved inspirational, what of the play

itself? The style of the drama was influenced by Maeterlinck, the Belgian Flemish writer who also wrote in French. Maeterlinck was a leading light in the Symbolist movement in continental Europe. He praised the play. Symbolism may be seen by critics as an affectation of style. Critical reputations are notoriously subject to fashion rather than reason.

Salomé is a play that needs to be played rather than read. The atmosphere is supposed to be built up by the introductory conversation amongst sentries and servants. On the page this dialogue is risible, improbable:

> *The Page of Herodias*: Look at the moon! How strange the moon seems! She is like a woman rising from a tomb. She is like a dead woman. You would fancy she was looking for dead things!'

The play is established through these characters until the main action of the play takes over when Salomé appears. She has power over men, due to her beauty through which she induces a young Syrian to let her see and speak to the Prophet. She touches the Prophet and makes clear her desire for him which he rejects, seeing her as the embodiment of evil. The drama of Salomé's meeting with Jokanaan is reinforced by the young Syrian killing himself: ' … and falls between Salomé and Jokanaan'. She cannot bear Jokanaan's rejection: the young Syrian is of no real consequence to her. Again on the page, this is inexplicable

– acted it becomes feasible. The Syrian's death is referred to later by Herodias' page in a touching little speech:

> … He was my brother, and nearer to me than a brother. I gave him a little box full of perfumes, and a ring of agate that he wore always on his hand. In the evening we used to walk by the river, among the almond trees, and he would tell me of the things of his country … He spake ever very low. The sound of his voice was like the sound of a flute, of a flute player. Also he much loved to gaze at himself in the river. I used to reproach him for that …

Why dwell on this? It is a counterpoint to the lusts of Herod, Herodias and Salomé. It represents what love is – and for Wilde it is significant that it is also the love between men. It is one touch of tenderness in a play dominated by lust and violence. It acknowledges too the narcissistic nature of love and admiration – which occurs elsewhere in Wilde's plays: see especially *The Importance of being Earnest*.

Herod's and Herodias' entourage come on to the scene. Again there are references to the moon by these characters. Wilde wants to build tension through repetitive references to the moon by different characters. This is weak stuff: but where the idea of repetition takes hold and dominates is when Salomé asks Herod for the head of Jokanaan, which he is clearly afraid to grant. Herod would offer anything but that:

... Listen. I have jewels hidden in this place – jewels that your mother even has never seen; jewels that are marvellous. I have a collar of pearls, set in four rows. They are like fifty moons caught in a golden net. On the ivory of her breast a queen has worn it ... I have amethysts of two kinds; one that is black like wine, and one that is red like wine which has been coloured with water. I have topazes yellow as are the eyes of tigers ... and beryls and chrysopases and rubies ... sardonyx and hyacinth stones and stones of chalcedony ...

In a sense, this feels like a reworking of Lord Henry Wotton's powers of seduction in *Dorian Gray* except that Herod's grossness is apparent.

The suspension of disbelief, as much as catharsis, is the essence of a tragic play's success. The former is the prerequisite of the latter. The action of this play, being in far-off times in strange lands, gives wider scope for the suspension of disbelief, but this would not by itself be enough. How is the play saved from itself? The answer lies in the powerful story line. Quibbles are overcome again by the central idea that a prophet of God would be swept away by the vengeful whim of a rejected girl on the back of the desire of an aged lecher. This is what makes the play. The death of Salomé caused by a fit of revulsion adds to, but does not redeem, the realisation that passions may lead people to do practically anything.

Despite the poetical, resplendent speeches, however

improbable, the action is brutal and direct. It is almost as if two stories are being told at once. It is flawed, bold and hypnotic. That is why it has survived.

Salomé and the minor plays represent one strand in Wilde's development as a playwright. He was inclined to think highly of them – as he did of his stories – because he could use them directly to test out ideas. The appeal of *Salomé* is probably greater outside the English-speaking world since it proposes ideas on a grand scale. It fits with Wilde's use of religious themes to make controversial ideas both acceptable and yet subversive. The sexual motive and the desire to use power are connected. Both lead to perverse, destructive outcomes.

By contrast, the stereotypical English mentality prefers humour and optimism, and thrives on indirect rather than direct reference. It is a mentality that shies away from the big picture. H.H. Munro understood this, suggesting that when the archangel Gabriel came to earth and set foot in England to announce Armageddon he is met with the reply 'It can't be! It is three days to Henley.' Wilde could supply wit and humour and through these means take the fight into the camp of the enemy. As a consequence, Wilde's serious dramas are overshadowed amongst English speakers by his comedies, almost to the point where it is a puzzle how Wilde would come to write them.

8

The Main Plays

Lady Windermere's Fan

'ANYONE CAN WRITE AN OSCAR WILDE play,' Wilde said ruefully, reflecting both his annoyance about the lack of appreciation of what was actually different about his work – and the oft-repeated criticism of being over-influenced by, if not actually plagiarising, the work of others. His attempts at playwriting had not been successful until *Lady Windermere's Fan*. There are hallmarks of a tentative enterprise about this particular play: initially, Wilde seems scarcely to have troubled himself. Lady Windermere (as a name) first appears in 'Lord Arthur Savile's Crime' – the most accomplished of Wilde's stories – and some of the dialogue is from *Dorian Gray*. If he is to be accused of plagiarism, it is from his own work. The aim was frankly commercial – could he recycle what he had already done for a profit? But he also craved success in the theatre. He wanted to be 'more witty than Congreve', as he put it in *De Profundis*.

The final product of this somewhat equivocal foray is *Lady Windermere's Fan* – as we know it, though it is a different thing from the original project. It is the result of collaboration between Wilde and George Alexander, the actor-manager of the St James's Theatre. Alexander commissioned Wilde with an advance of £100 – then a very considerable sum. Wilde took his time in writing it and was ambiguous about it – at one stage saying that it was 'lifeless', as he says in his *Letters*, and was apt to disdain it as 'one of those modern drawing-room plays with pink lampshades'. By the time he and Alexander had finished with it (Alexander knew how to stage a play, and Wilde did not) Alexander was so pleased that he offered to buy the copyright for £1,000. Wilde's business acumen led him to turn down the proposal, guessing that if Alexander offered that sum it must be worth more. And so it proved: it was a commercial success and really launched Wilde's career as a dramatist.

Windermere is set socially amongst the leisured, moneyed and aristocratic classes whose concerns are to maintain the edifices of social custom and conventional morality with the attendant hypocrisy of saying one thing and doing another. They had the time and, significantly, the money and inclination to go to plays that depicted them-selves – an interesting aspect of narcissism. These classes of people had the time and energy for such games: it all helped maintain social distinctions – the class 'system' and their position in that structure. Why should that be important? It was the engine of survival and prosperity (not what you know, but who you know and what they can do for you). Slightly differently expressed, it is still true today. Underneath these social structures, though, people are, despite all appearances, human: they have desires which perforce they must enact. These contrasts and contradictions are Wilde's subject matter. He was able to write about them because they were the driving force of his own creativity: he needed also to reach reconciliation of these opposing forces. The consequence of the interplay between social manoeuvring, and the underlying truth is the ever-present threat of disclosure, scandal and social disgrace which then bars the person discovered from 'society'. The loss of social position – from which everything seemed to flow – is a form of death sentence. *Windermere* is the first of Wilde's plays to deal with this set of issues in the form of comedy. The play of wit in this play, *A Woman of No Importance* and *An Ideal Husband* makes these plays seem to be comedies of manners – except for the dramatic episodes in all three – all related to the fear of discovery and scandal, where there is a strong element of sentimentality. Adultery, infidelity and the notion of good character that may not be impugned – but runs a high risk of being accused of these social crimes – provide the dramatic force of these plays. In all three plays there is the handling of the consequences of passion, the threat of scandal and exclusion from society. Acknowledged roués and sinners turn out to be saviours; they can after all continue to be adulterers, people of easy virtue, but they can more easily take the blame; thus the main characters may continue their lives. This overturns conventional wisdom. There has to be a happy reconciliation – it is a comedy after all. The negative aspect from the standpoint of art is that the same ingredients make up melodrama. There are scenes that skate dangerously close to it. The only play in which this potential defect is overcome is *The Importance of Being Earnest*.

In terms of artistic development, *Windermere* stands in a direct relation to *Vera*. Both plays have a serious theme: and both have wit interspersed, but in *Windermere* the force of social observation generates the play's momentum and the vehicle for wit. Wilde's wit arises from observation and his critique of society, which is derived from, and illustrates, his world view.

The question posed by *Windermere* is: how are passion and the truth about passion to be accommodated within existing social conventions? People who play by the rules of the game pay the price of denying their true feelings, and those that do not become social outcasts. They need reconciliation and forgiveness. Mrs Erlynne says: 'Ideals are dangerous things. Realities are better. They wound, but they are better.' Characteristically, Wilde is of both parties. He enjoys the depiction of the shallowness and greed of the Duchess of Berwick, who marries off her daughter to Mr Hopper, a rich Australian whose 'vulgarity' is excused completely by his wealth. In the marriage market, designed to preserve or gain wealth, love or indeed considerations of taste, shared interests or any other supposed bond of mutual interest are not the consideration. Love has to follow material comfort and social position – if it is to be viable at all. In the final analysis, this denial of love and finer feelings is, if not impossible, destructive. This is demonstrated in the action of the play. Wilde's ironic detachment from the marriage market, brought about in turn by his detachment from his heterosexual nature, enabled him to see, more clearly and wittily but distantly, the relations between men and women, and also critically, the games that women have to play to survive. This may present itself as a limitation, but it makes the play, as well as the other comedies, so entertaining. Wilde's world view was that the conflict between the ideal and the real, between opposites, led to a truer understanding of the world. This analysis applied to property and the marriage market versus fundamental passions. For Wilde, following (as ever) ancient Greek ideas about the gods being personifications of those passions, the gods are not mocked – and their vengeance is palpable. Thence the passions are fundamental and cannot without peril be repressed or ignored.

Act 1 establishes these themes, the people and, in the first few lines, the fan – which is a gift from Lord Windermere to Lady Windermere, who has just come of age. Serious themes are discussed in a conversation with Lord Darlington, who interrupts a scene of domestic bliss: Lady Windermere is pruning some roses. Their conversation is wide-ranging but revolves around Lady Windermere. She says: 'I lived always with Lady Julia, my father's elder sister, you know. She was stern to me, but she taught me what the world is forgetting, the difference that there is between what is right and what is wrong. She allowed of no compromise. I allow of none.'

She continues: 'Nowadays people seem to look on life as a speculation. It is not a speculation. It is a sacrament. Its ideal is Love. Its purification is sacrifice.'

This lofty talk – which the play as a whole will put to the test, is challenged right away by the worldly Lord Darlington, who provides a conversational instance where a woman might be forgiven for repaying her husband's infidelity with infidelity of her own. Lady Windermere resists this idea vehemently. Lord Darlington replies: 'Do you know that I am afraid that good people do a great deal of harm in this world.' There then follows an almost Socratic dialogue between the two where Lord Darlington draws her out on her attitude to sexual infidelity, about which she is clear and rigid, whilst admitting to her his own latitudinarianism: 'I think life too complex a thing to be settled by these hard and fast rules.'

When the Duchess of Berwick arrives with her daughter the dialogue becomes more light-hearted, filling out the details of the social scene they both inhabit including a dance to be held in Lady Windermere's honour. After Lord Darlington leaves, the true purpose of the Duchess' visit is disclosed. The Duchess tells Lady Windermere that Mrs Erlynne ('that horrid woman') has some private connection with Lord Windermere: 'I have been told that this woman has got a great deal of money out of somebody, for it seems that she came to London six months ago without anything at all to speak of, and now she has this charming house in Mayfair, drives her ponies in the Park every afternoon and all – well, all – since she has known poor dear Windermere.'

After the Duchess' departure, Lady Windermere goes through her husband's chequebook and is able to confirm that he has given large sums of money to Mrs Erlynne. Convinced by the Duchess' story, when Lord Windermere returns, she challenges him. Windermere's responses are evasive and unpersuasive. Lady Windermere concludes unsurprisingly, that Mrs Erlynne is a courtesan: 'Oh, don't imagine I mind about the money … But what I do mind is that you who have loved me, you who have taught me to love you, should pass from the love that is given to the love that is bought.'

He simply says that it is not as it appears. He asks Lady Windermere to invite Mrs Erlynne to her dance – so as to restore Mrs Erlynne's social standing. She has committed an unnamed social indiscretion:

'I tell you simply this – Mrs Erlynne was once honoured, loved, respected. She was well born, she had position – she lost everything – threw it away, if you like. That makes it all the more bitter. Misfortunes one can endure – they come from outside, they are accidents. But to suffer for one's own faults – ah! – there is the sting of life …'

This is a philosophical comment: there are 'substance' or 'essence' and 'accidents': what you *are*, is to be differentiated from what *happens* to you, and this is a direct reference to Wilde's views of human nature. It is hardly satisfying to Lady Windermere, who rejects any suggestion that she would invite Mrs Erlynne to her house. When her husband does, she threatens a scene. Act 1 closes with Lord Windermere saying to the audience: 'My God! What shall I do? I dare not tell her who this woman really is. The shame would kill her.' Lord Windermere is in a dilemma – he wants to do the 'right' thing, but the right thing is socially and personally damaging – and that, also, would be 'wrong'. In the prevailing concept of polite society such candour would represent a departure from social norms and would not be forgiven.

Act 2 is set at Lady Windermere's ball. The tension here is built around Lady Windermere, the Windermeres' marriage and Mrs Erlynne. Will Mrs Erlynne come to the party to celebrate Lady Windermere's coming of age? She cannot help but come for this reason. Other characters are diverting but also contributing to the tension of the occasion. The Duchess of Berwick is preparing her daughter to be affianced to the wealthy Australian Mr Hopper. The Duchess indicates her view of her daughter, who seems in her unmarried state an encumbrance, merely a commodity to be procured by Hopper's riches. In exchange, Hopper gets a young wife and a chance of social standing which the Duchess, symbolising the attitude of her social class, is making a show of being reluctant to grant. The Duchess has terms: her daughter is to be set up in state and in London as a respectable member of society, and definitely not Australia where Hopper has made his fortune.

The habitual niceties of such vapid occasions are described in the character of Mr Dumby, who wanders around the crowd pandering to those who are socially significant: Lady Stutfield and the Duchess. Mrs Cowper-Cowper is treated differently according to his perceptions of her lesser social standing. This is the game that is being played – according to the rules. The rules are laughed at but in reality, they are despicable and dehumanising. In the major action of the play the same rules if infringed bring about scandal and shame – followed by social ostracism.

Lord Augustus, who is the ingénu, arrives. He is fascinated by Mrs Erlynne, and puzzled by the reaction of other women to her. He is open, pragmatic and straightforward in a world that is quite simply not. He is the butt of other people's remarks, but is, finally, impervious to them.

Mrs Erlynne's long-anticipated entrance to the ball makes her the focus of attention – society has to deal with her. She takes the initiative, introducing herself to Lady Windermere, who is cold to her. In turn, Lady Windermere quickly seeks solace in the company of Lord Darlington, who eagerly receives her. He wants her for himself. Lady Windermere's actions stand in contrast to her declaration of ideals: she is the wronged woman who must get revenge.

In seeking solace in the company of Lord Darlington she is making an error. This becomes clear when, contrary to his declarations of friendship in Act 1, he says: 'Between men and women there is no friendship possible. There is passion, enmity, worship, love, but no friendship. I love you!' The unstated reason is sexual attraction. The moment of drama is compounded by her rejection of his advances. He increases the pressure: 'My life, my whole life. Take it … do with it what you will … ' She concedes that she lacks the courage, to which Darlington responds: 'Be yourself!' and she says: 'I am afraid of being myself … ' And there in a nutshell is the Wildean point of view. Physical attraction entails polarisation of feelings; the steadfastness of friendship seems milk and water by comparison. Being yourself requires courage to defy convention, but is also folly.

In the meantime, Mrs Erlynne's plan to re-enter society seems to be working well. She achieves an introduction to some of the minor women through her influence over men.

Mrs Erlynne knows how to handle men: dealing with women is altogether more formidable. She gains acceptance of the grandest of them all, Lady Berwick. Lady Berwick announces to Lady Windermere: 'I am so sorry for what I said to you this afternoon about her … Of course, she must be all right if *you* invite her.' Other parts of her plan are revealed too: to marry Lord Augustus and to get Lord Windermere to make a settlement on her. Mrs Erlynne's character appears to be opportunistic, unattractive, grasping and set.

Mrs Erlynne's acceptance into society compounds Lady Windermere's sense of humiliation and spurs her to accept Lord Darlington's offer. She leaves a letter for her husband – and goes off in search of Lord Darlington. When the worldly Mrs Erlynne discovers Lady Windermere has left the house, she quickly discerns what has happened. She finds the letter and opens it. In a soliloquy, she discloses that she is Lady Windermere's mother, and that she had made a similar error of judgement twenty years before. She then wants to protect her child from the same folly: 'does life repeat its tragedies?'. She is determined to prevent the same fate befalling her daughter and tells Lord Augustus to detain the men at the club so that Lord Windermere does not realise that his wife has left home.

Act 3 opens in Lord Darlington's rooms with a soliloquy from Lady Windermere, which is interrupted by Mrs Erlynne's arrival. Mrs Erlynne urges her to leave: 'You are on the brink of ruin.' She finally prevails, in a scene that requires the suspension of disbelief, only for the men to arrive. The only resort is for them both to hide, to save their reputations. Lady Windermere forgets to gather up the fan. The men start a conversation – about women, which is the excuse for verbal sparring. Lord Augustus is the butt of much of the badinage: the innocent amongst the worldly. In fact, he is pivotal to the play's resolution: he is what you see – twice divorced, candid about his needs, to find the right partner. Such characters are the stock in trade of comedy – easily gulled but easily satisfied with the potential to be truly happy. This is the inversion of John Stuart Mill's 'Better to be Socrates dissatisfied than a fool satisfied.' The repartee which is extended is the occasion for Wilde to drop in his aphorisms, which have since become endlessly quoted. Verbal sparring amongst the menfolk gives a homoerotic slant to the scene, which is less noticed in a male-dominated society. Martin Seymour-Smith once said to me that Wilde would have liked to write as Joe Orton did in a much different epoch. Perhaps he did, but using different conventions. Commercial playwriting requires that an audience is prepared to leave home and pay for what they see and hear – there would have been little or no West End audience for an overtly homoerotic play.

All is well until Lord Windermere sees his wife's fan. He immediately suspects her of being in Darlington's rooms, Darlington of course hopes that is the case – but can't afford a confrontation. Mrs Erlynne comes into the room; she has the least to lose in terms of reputation, but the most to protect – her daughter. The ensuing consternation enables her daughter to leave unobserved. Lord Augustus is the only character who feels aggrieved. Everyone else is knowing and smug.

Act 4 ties things together. The morning after a party is a time to ponder the events of the night before: again it opens with a soliloquy by Lady Windermere wondering what transpired after she left Darlington's room. Would Mrs Erlynne sacrifice her reputation to save hers? The answer to this question is given in her husband's demeanour. She and Windermere resolve to leave town. She wants to see Mrs Erlynne before they leave. Windermere is against the idea: 'she is inadmissible anywhere.' Mrs Erlynne arrives and is received by Lady Windermere before this difference of opinion becomes definitive. Lady Windermere is pleased to see her – and is dismayed by learning that Mrs Erlynne is due to leave the country permanently. She leaves the room to fetch a photograph of herself and her son for Mrs Erlynne. Immediately Mrs Erlynne and Windermere confront one another. There are no holds barred. The fundamental issue is whether or not to tell Lady Windermere that Mrs Erlynne is her mother. In this power game Mrs Erlynne's bad reputation is the trump card: and she is prepared to use it. She will decide. When Lady Windermere returns there follows a discussion about her knowledge of her mother and her father's way of dealing with what was actually a scandal. In this engagement the women's differing viewpoints come into the open:

> *Lady Windermere*: We all have ideals in life. At least we all should have. Mine is my mother.
> *Mrs Erlynne*: Ideals are dangerous things. Realities are better. They wound, but they're better.
> *Lady Windermere*: If I lost my ideals, I should lose everything.

This remark decides Mrs Erlynne not to disclose her relationship to her daughter.

Just as she is about to leave, Lord Augustus arrives. He is no match for Mrs Erlynne's force of character. She makes him escort her to her carriage. And her native wit invents a plausible narrative to explain her presence in Darlington's rooms, which he gleefully accepts 'She is just the woman for me. Suits me down to the ground.' He is to marry her. Everyone, for quite different reasons is pleased.

The argument is for the necessity of illusions, and as a consequence of that, the necessity of masks. The play is essentially about private acceptance of some things inherent in people, but public portrayal of something else which is socially acceptable. Each member of the audience as if alone, is let into the play's secrets. This picture of reality acknowledges the forces that shape human lives – essentially the passions that drive us – and the events that then follow.

It explores the way we deal with these – denial and subterfuge, and postulates compromise in the interests of the greater good, which is defined as the greater happiness. It is a curiously Utilitarian philosophy.

Considered solely as a play, *Windermere* relies rather too heavily on soliloquy to move things forward. The mixture of melodrama, wit and humour tending towards a sense of happiness at the play's close makes it a comedy, but considered as comedy there are heavy-handed episodes. As a 'serious' play, it has too much amusement. It is playable possibly because of this strange blend of seriousness and laughter.

A Woman of No Importance

A Woman of No Importance followed relatively quickly on from *Windermere*: if a playwright can produce one successful popular play, where is the next? This is the commercial theatre, after all. The play is in one sense more technically accomplished than *Windermere*. Wilde is getting into his stride: he can write something the public demonstrably wants, and he can be more fluent. *A Woman* is set in the same social milieu as *Windermere*.

Yet despite the flaws in *Windermere*, *A Woman* lacks its appeal. The reason for this is to do with the plot, which concerns another woman who is outside society: Mrs Arbuthnot, this time not seeking an entrée – another victim of sexual passion as a result of which she has a son, Gerald, to whom she is devoted. To protect herself and her son she has withdrawn from society, in order to bring him up. At the time of the action of the play her son is a young man on the brink of a promising career in politics. He is in love with an idealistic, young and rich American girl, Hester, who is an orphan – that is to say, another outsider. Mrs Arbuthnot is drawn back into society because of her talented (and adoring) son. Gerald's career in politics has made a promising start. This career would become brilliant: he has the offer of a secretaryship to Lord Illingworth, a Dandy, an unmarried roué and a leading political figure, cynical and worldly-wise. Once she learns this, she is horrified – Illingworth is her former lover and her son's father and represents everything that she wants her son not to be. The truth about Illingworth and Gerald's paternity is forced out by circumstances. Gerald in effect has to choose between his father and his mother. The dilemma is resolved by Illingworth making a pass at Hester. The son can thus turn down Illingworth's offer, stay true to his mother's love, and at the same time have the love of Hester.

For a man not to leave his mother takes on a different meaning from a woman's self-sacrifice as in *Windermere*. It is also as close a description of Wilde's situation as any. Wilde adored his mother and disapproved of his father's conduct to his mother, whilst worshipping her for her fortitude and humanity in dealing with his father. Constance is the idealist, approved of by Lady Wilde, and

Constance finds solace in Lady Wilde's friendship – she becomes the mother that Constance has always wanted. Gerald is both heterosexual and mother-fixated, or indeed homosexual.

The role of Illingworth as Dandy is worth considering too: he is self-admiring, witty and above all selfish and uncaring. He has no really admirable qualities, and his self-seeking is his undoing. Wilde's admiration for, and emulation of, Dandies is deconstructed: Wilde's thought is never what it appears to be.

An Ideal Husband

Part, and not the least part, of a play is its title: it must draw the right crowd to pay to see it. *An Ideal Husband* immediately interests everyone – those who would be sentimental, or cynical, or the troubled, as well as those who are merely curious about the institution of marriage. Wilde was all of those things. The play is set at the highest levels of society, so it is also fashionable. The dramatist has then to carry it off so that there is a never-ending supply of audiences. Wilde had proved he could do just that.

But for Wilde, a play could not just be formulaic: it had to deal with 'real' things as well – his preoccupation with relationships, the power of fundamental emotions and how these affect relationships, the tensions that the institution of marriage brings, the need for love and the improbability of spontaneous love in marriage. Marriage requires the adoption of civic roles: husband, wife, father, mother, in-laws and so forth. Social expectations and desires so often are on a collision course, as Wilde knew: he could look at his own marriage and that of his parents. Marriage was (and is) also a property relationship. In Wilde's day this was especially pronounced. Women and men of a certain social class had property settled on them to help secure their future – maintain or improve the social standing of their family. A good match was not so much one of personal compatibilities but one of property. This was seen so often as the precondition of marriage happening at all. In Jane Austen's *Pride and Prejudice* Mrs Bennet can talk of little else. In the poorer sections of society – in Thomas Hardy's rural England – agricultural labourers, amongst the poorest working people in the land, sold their wives at country fairs when they could no longer support them. It is not so difficult to see in these circumstances why questions can arise: how is love possible? or to be realised? or how should people regard their life partner? or should they see them as life partners? These are poignant questions for everyone – the more so because they need to be asked, no less than in the answer that may result. The cheerful resignation of the Cockney rhyming slang for wife, 'trouble and strife', is matched by females asking 'why are there no good men about?'

George Bernard Shaw, critic, playwright and self-appointed seer, Wilde's contemporary, thought that *An*

Ideal Husband was Wilde's best play: 'In a certain sense Mr Wilde is to me our only thorough playwright. He plays with everything: with wit, with philosophy, with drama, with actors and audience, with the whole theatre.' Shaw did not like *The Importance of Being Earnest* so well – he thought it was mechanical and could have been written 'ten years before'. In an important sense he was right. *Husband* walks down the high road of the life of contemporary high society – marriage and social standing against the underlying reality, political office and corruption, love and friendship and the meaning of these. Everyone has guilt of some kind, which accounts for behaviour: lying, concealment, avoidance and so on. Wilde addressed himself to the ruling elite, and the social pretensions that are never far from a hierarchical society. Scandals of corruption, divorce, adultery and sexual deviancy amongst members of the ruling class rocked Victorian society and ended careers; in modulated ways the same happens now. The other reason why he addressed himself to this class of person was simple: they were avid theatregoers with money, and liked, as everybody does, to be 'talked about'.

If *Lady Windermere's Fan* is reconstructed from Wilde's novel and short stories (*Dorian Gray* and *Lord Arthur Savile's Crime*) into a play, then *An Ideal Husband* is a play aspiring to be a novel. Consider the stage directions and descriptions of character, which are very full:

… Mrs Marchmont and Lady Basildon, two very pretty women, are seated together on a Louis Seize sofa. They are types of exquisite fragility. Their affectation of manner has a delicate charm. Watteau would have loved to paint them.

… Mabel Chiltern is a perfect example of the English type of prettiness, the apple-blossom type. She has all the fragrance and freedom of a flower. [Note Wilde's alliteration – meant to be savoured, but by whom?]

There is ripple after ripple of sunlight in her hair, and the little mouth, with its parted lips, is expectant, like the mouth of a child. She has the fascinating tyranny of youth, and the astonishing courage of innocence. To sane people she is not reminiscent of any work of art. But she is really like a Tanagra statuette, and would be rather annoyed if she were told so …

Sir Robert Chiltern: ' … a personality of mark. Not popular – few personalities are. But intensely admired by the few, and deeply respected by the many … It would be inaccurate to call him picturesque. Picturesqueness cannot survive the House of Commons. But van Dyck would have liked to have painted his head … '

Wilde's preoccupations with art and its interplay with life are evident from the references to Tanagra figurines, Watteau, and van Dyck, as well as the descriptions of stage settings, where life imitates art and vice versa. The aesthete in him is not a mere badge or affectation – it really is how Wilde views art (in this case drama), and through that medium, life. The creed of aestheticism, whether of art or morals, is too narrow to survive even the practice of art, as his plays amply show. The animation and liveliness that Wilde is able to impart to his characters as they play out the drama, suggest a wider, actually moral canvas. This is to do with the notions of the necessity of transgression (sin), the corresponding need for understanding, forgiveness, compassion and acceptance.

Sir Robert Chiltern's corrupt past dealings are in contrast to his reputation, which is not just public in the sense that scandal might dislodge it, but private too – where he would risk losing his wife's gushing esteem, and thence, love. What she loves is an image of her husband, an idealisation – perhaps what he would have wished to have been, not the real man who by reference to the ideal, is flawed.

On a more general level, the contrast of the ideal with the actual returns to Wilde's philosophical view: in a Platonic way the ideal or 'form' of, say, beauty is derived by a process of abstraction from the many instances of beautiful things and people, but that form itself is not available to perception. Perception only delivers individual instances, which are always flawed. This difficulty is distinctly Wildean: the idea or 'form' of a husband might have all the desirable attributes of a loving nature, honour, fidelity and so forth. The reality of husbands is another thing. How then, are we to reconcile the one with the other? This is the theme of the play.

The action of the play is fluid, establishing itself initially in the dialogue of two aristocratic ladies who have nothing better to do than languidly go to parties – in this case a political party at the Chilterns', to alleviate their boredom. The young Lady Chiltern is referred to as some earnest young person who believes that everyone should have a serious purpose in life – which is why they have come to the party, whilst doubting it: 'I don't see anybody here to-night whom one could possibly call a serious purpose.'

The rapid and easy movement of the play continues as another central character, Lord Goring, is introduced obliquely by his father, Lord Caversham, asking after his son whom he describes as a 'good for nothing'. The young Mabel Chiltern, Sir Robert's young sister, challenges Caversham's description of his son as idle by riposting un-ironically with a string of pleasures (opera, horse riding, etc) with which Goring occupies himself.

Mrs Cheveley, who is to wreak such destruction, also attends the party, recently arrived from Vienna. Lady Chiltern knows her from schooldays and is repelled by her. Sir Robert Chiltern enters and is drawn into conversation with Mrs Cheveley. He is formal whilst she is worldly-wise.

Goring's attendance is well flagged by the time he arrives: he is charming, witty and seemingly a friend to everyone. He knows Mrs Cheveley. After dinner, Mrs Cheveley's purpose is made clear: to promote the Argentine Canal Company scheme which Chiltern regards as a 'commonplace

Stock Exchange swindle'. Chiltern intends to speak in the House of Commons denouncing the scheme. Mrs Cheveley asks him not do this, the threat being that she has evidence that he has made his fortune corruptly. He does not want to comply – but the threat of blackmail, scandal and ruin persuades him temporarily not to denounce the scheme. Alone with his wife they discuss Mrs Cheveley who Lady Chiltern claims was a one-time thief. Mrs Cheveley is boasting that Chiltern will support the scheme. This horrifies the idealistic Lady Chiltern whose counter-threat is that Chiltern will lose her love if he gives in to Mrs Cheveley's wishes.

Goring moves to centre stage in Act 2. He has a special role as the figure about whom the play begins to turn. He is lovingly described. He is the link amongst all the characters – he has had an affair with Mrs Cheveley and is the passionate friend of the Chilterns, for whom he is a safe confidant. He is capable of love though unattached. An 'ideal' person from quite another point of view, he is a Dandy with the gift of ironic social detachment. Significantly, when Chiltern and Goring discuss Chiltern's predicament, Goring says:

> *Goring*: I had no idea that you, of all men in the world, could have been so weak, Robert, as to yield to such a temptation as Baron Arnheim held out to you.
> *Chiltern*: Weak? Oh, I am sick of hearing that phrase. Sick of using it about others. Weak? Do you really think,

Arthur, that it is weakness that yields to temptation? I tell you that there are terrible temptations that it requires strength, strength and courage, to yield to.

This inversion of conventional thinking is the Wildean perception of the risks that must be taken in order to be yourself. This is the meaning of temptation: it really is the indicator of the fundamental truths of your personality. Chiltern wanted to be rich in order to be a political leader, and a corrupt deal was a quick way of achieving it. Yielding to temptation is thus a bold act. The consequences are visited on him by the close of Act 2: his wife rejects him once she learns from Mrs Cheveley that his fortune was built up from money dishonestly obtained by selling a secret.

In Act 3, Goring moves definitively to centre stage. The act opens with a dialogue between Goring and Phipps, his manservant. This is one of the origins of the Wooster/Jeeves type of relationship – where the servant is given the impassive but all-knowing, role. (This idea is developed further in *The Importance of Being Earnest*.) It is a light relief before the mood changes swiftly as the problem of what Chiltern is to do to regain the love of his wife surfaces once more. Goring manages to manipulate Mrs Cheveley into surrendering the letter by suggesting that she has stolen a fine bracelet. Mrs Cheveley retaliates by stealing Lady Chiltern's letter to him. This letter is an appeal for help from Lady Chiltern but could be read as signifying a passionate affair. Mrs Cheveley intends to send it to Chiltern.

Act 4 opens with Goring in centre stage again – this time in dialogue with his father, Lord Caversham, who expects him to marry, and then with Mabel Chiltern with whom he is in love. Goring is obliged to tell Lady Chiltern about the letter stolen by Mrs Cheveley. Chiltern has by this time denounced the Argentinian Canal scheme. The loose end is Lady Chiltern's letter. This is cleared up by being opened by the wrong person and handed to Chiltern who believes it to be addressed to him. Lady Chiltern tells him that Goring has destroyed the letter revealing Chiltern's misconduct which Mrs Cheveley was using to blackmail him. He promises to give up public life to please her. It would appear that it only remains for Goring to ask Chiltern to allow him to marry Mabel. Chiltern initially denies this request – because of Goring's racy character. Lady Chiltern then confesses that her letter was addressed to Goring, and that in fact she did not go to him. In a rush the Goring/Mabel match is agreed. Lady Chiltern relents on Chiltern's withdrawal from public life. It is concluded that genuine love, which entails forgiveness, can overcome all obstacles. Seemingly order is restored.

On this framework ideas about politics, life, marriage, Dandyism are placed. Any weakness of plot is overcome by the momentum of the dialogue, a mixture of wit, humour as well as pathos, fear and disdain.

The title is *An Ideal Husband*, but the play becomes a

portrait of the ideal man: a man of taste and discrimination, wit and humour, who is candid about his weaknesses and yet has honour. The play's hero is Lord Goring, who is an upgraded version of Lord Henry Wotton and the man that Wilde would have liked to be. *An Ideal Husband* is the most fluent of the plays until *The Importance of Being Earnest.*

The Importance of Being Earnest

Playgoers love *The Importance of Being Earnest* and, as with all worthwhile plays, its appeal crosses the generations as well as the sexual orientations of people. Whatever in-crowd joke there was in the title (being 'earnest' also meant being attracted to one's own sex), this is an aside and not what the play is about. Playing the play *à la* Genet with all male actors is an absurd affectation. Both men and women in the play are as vivid and distinctive as the style of the play allows: they are not men disguised as women. The play is about the pursuit of love and the effect it has on people. The poet Earl of Rochester describes the state as a 'happy ruin'.

Despite taking place in the milieu of the moneyed, leisured aristocratic classes – that intensely connected group, it manages to transcend its immediate context. Everyone has a social position and a set of rules that have to be observed – so the imaginative leap is not that great. It is about love, deception and disclosure, which everyone knows about. It can then cheerfully ask the audience to suspend disbelief, which they do. The play has a resemblance to *Engaged* by W.S. Gilbert, and there is Gilbertian influence on its style: this is the reference that Bernard Shaw is making. W.S. Gilbert wrote what he called 'burlesques' or 'entertainments' as we would now say. As ever, Wilde's use of a model is the start, not the end of the story: it is the framework on which he wants to hang his observations and to spell out his philosophical viewpoint.

What an audience sees in the play is not necessarily what Wilde intended. He was amused by his play. Yet he claimed that liking *Earnest* was one way of disliking his work. It is more subtle than, yet as full of intrigue as, his other work. It is a social commentary of a gentler kind. The play describes the marriage market as well as romance. It is amongst other things a sustained piece of persiflage. Unlike his other comedies there are no melodramatic scenes and lofty declarations. The contrast could not be greater between the earlier work and this last play.

The play is a sophisticated demonstration of what Wilde thought human nature is generally, but especially when in love. Part of that story is that, in needing love we project that feeling on to another person, whereupon the fantasy begins. Much effort is expended on making ourselves into that imaginary being that we think so desirable to others. This deception is mutual. *Earnest* explores this almost solipsistic world – that is the world of all lovers. Much of it is also a self-deception, for what is sought is real love that accepts us as we are, not as we pretend to be.

The play is thus also one about masks: a favourite theme of Wilde's. The truth is disclosed in the mask(s) that we choose. Wilde knew about masks – he had to wear one such in order to live: his tragedy is that when the mask fell from him he was hypocritically vilified. This play enters into that difficult territory. No one is exactly who they appear to be, with the exception of Lady Bracknell and the girls – Gwendolen and Cecily. Lady Bracknell upholds the social norms (very largely those of the connections that a person has) of Society on the basis that this is what one should do, and in so doing acknowledges one's limitations. Exceptions to the social norms may be made within limits, especially when wealth comes into consideration, which is itself another kind of norm. She is the spiritual descendant of Jane Austen's Mrs Bennet except that she has genuine authority and no pretensions to anything she is not. She is a social reductionist, expecting no more of life than it can give, disliking change because it is nearly always for the worse. She is a satire on the nature of the ruling class, its pretensions and limitations.

The girls, Gwendolen and Cecily on the other hand, are just as straightforward as Lady Bracknell but starting out on life they have different objectives. Their purpose is to have the things that girls of their station have a right to expect: romance, engagement, marriage to someone of their choice who is socially acceptable and with the means to support the lifestyle they need. Some critics seem to think that this amounts to masculinisation of these characters. This is simply not so. Wilde uses the women in his plays and works generally to make shrewd and most often subversive observations. It should be remembered that Wilde's mother as well as his wife had independence of thought. Lady Wilde was a fervent Irish Nationalist; and Constance Wilde was a vocal supporter of women's rights. Both were highly intelligent people and both were authors.

Masks are embodied in the form of Jack Worthing – Jack in the Country, Ernest in Town. Jack is a pillar of society in the country but he needs the Ernest figure (the name he uses in town) who he pretends is his miscreant brother whom he has to get out of scrapes. Jack is enabled thus to go to town to lead a freer life. His friend Algernon is as much a schemer as Jack. Algernon has an imaginary friend called Bunbury of indifferent health who can call on him at a moment's notice, to enable Algernon to escape from the social round of London. 'Bunburyism' has entered the language. The characters' encounters with love, or perhaps more exactly the pursuit of love, unravels these deceptions. Algernon adopts the name Ernest and travels to the country to visit Jack but actually in pursuit of Cecily who intrigues him: this is the fission point of the play that eventually causes the fragile edifices of deception to collapse.

Practically all the characters in the play have things to hide: how they appear is not how they are, whether it is the governess Miss Prism or John Worthing. In desiring love, they have to come to terms with their past, that is themselves.

Analysis of social class underlies the play: it lies at the heart of Lady Bracknell's behaviour. The dramatis personae are the leisured classes, professionals (Dr Chasuble, the Anglican priest) and servants. Algernon and his servant Lane develop the relationship first charted by Goring and his manservant in *An Ideal Husband*. Lane is a detached, even wryly amused, character who is able to speak more direct truths to his employer and is quite unmoved by his master's pretensions.

As in Wilde's other comedies, all the characters are connected with one another over long periods of time. These connections are brought out gradually. The plot draws them together on a collision course. The resolution of this drama is the triumph of love over circumstances, although Wilde makes these circumstances melt away. He leaves things as they are. If money is required to make things work, he conjures it – here there is a resemblance to the short story 'The Model Millionaire'. If someone requires parentage, he supplies it. Borges' observation of Wilde's comedies as tending towards happiness as a theme is correct. This is another reason why audiences like the play. On the other hand, it is easy to see Shaw's irritation at the mechanical nature of the plot. Shaw preferred an Ibsenist rough house for his own plays. Wilde is undermining conventions rather than frontally attacking them.

9

Letters and Journalism

WILDE'S LETTERS WERE COLLECTED IN THE main edition of 1962 by Rupert Hart-Davis as simply *The Letters of Oscar Wilde*, and since that time other letters have come to light, and new editions have appeared. The point of reading letters is to bring the subject alive again and to get a perspective on the main written work. His letters on the whole have pace and are easy to read, and contain aperçus that bear memorising.

Wilde was a prolific letter writer. It is important to realise that many of his letters which might otherwise have been retained were lost because of the scandal of his personal life and the haste with which so many of his correspondents wished to distance themselves from him. He wrote to his wife daily whenever he was away yet few of these letters have survived. His letters were scattered far and wide, and some have reappeared even in recent years. The Hart-Davis edition contains also exceptionally useful footnotes that shed light on the recipients, many of whom are interesting in their own right, and collectively also on the culture and ethos of the age.

Nevertheless, Wilde's life and work can be traced through his letters. The nature of his prose varies: oscillating – between the unaffected and the purple, as it does elsewhere.

The *Letters* do not show, as might be supposed, a weary decadent, but a man full of energy, actively maintaining a network of friends, colleagues and associates. They also show that he had a tough mind when it came to business, especially securing new income (see his letter to Mary Anderson concerning his play *Guido Ferranti* in New York). His extravagance and resulting want of money is an important driving force in his life both as a man and as a writer. Dr Johnson thought that no man wrote except for money. Wilde would agree. 'I have been rich and I have been poor. Rich is better.' His letter to the Inspector of Taxes should be framed and put on the wall of tax offices to show the grinding effects that taxation professionals have on individual taxpayers:

> … I wish your notices were not so agitating and did not hold out such dreadful threats. A penalty of fifty pounds sounds like a relic of mediaeval torture. Your obedient servant …

There are letters that show him in pursuit of lovers, female as well as, mostly, male. His ambisexuality begins to emerge in his correspondence with the young undergraduate Harry Marillier. Then there are the letters to Robert Ross who first seduced him, but who remained a faithful friend and finally, became his literary executor. As he became more involved in the theatre the pace of life visibly quickens on all levels: business as well as pleasure. He had more sexual encounters and there are letters which amount to a brush-off of previous but now unwanted conquests.

De Profundis

The most substantial of his letters is that addressed to Lord Alfred Douglas (Bosie), his lover. It was published as *De Profundis* and was written towards the end of Wilde's prison term. From 1905 until Douglas' death in 1945 it was published in a heavily censored way so as to avoid litigation by Douglas. The full text has been available since then. This is very necessary, but a mixed blessing. Wilde's work always had a biographical element in it – but this was submerged. *De Profundis* is the polar opposite. Whereas the motivation to write for publication might arise from feelings, situations or insights – how the story is told is a different thing. With *De Profundis* the events themselves of Wilde's life are a significant part of the text. *De Profundis* invites perforce the reader to take sides in a love affair which has resulted in Wilde's social and financial ruin. The standing that Wilde had assiduously cultivated and latterly, through his work, justified, has been swept away in a courtroom. There was no possibility of secrecy. The evidence in the trials as Wilde put it was false, but the allegations against him were true. This was a calamity both for Wilde, and for his family. This and Douglas' neglect of him is the spur to write: he is expressing anguish and recrimination. It represents a meanness of spirit which he would otherwise deplore – but it is also cathartic. Catharsis is a function of art, but this is life, and is thus more difficult to script. It was written (and rewritten) over a period of three months (January–March 1897) prior to his release in May 1897. It was handed to Robert Ross to have typewritten copies made before forwarding it to Douglas – lest it be changed or destroyed. Wilde's anger and hurt feelings are to the fore:

> Our ill-fated and most lamentable friendship has ended in ruin and public infamy for me, yet the memory of our ancient affection is often with me, and the thought that loathing, bitterness and contempt should for ever take that place in my heart once held by love is very sad to me: and you yourself will, I think, feel in your heart that to write to me as I lie in the loneliness of prison-life is better than to publish my letters without my permission or to dedicate poems to me unasked, though the world will know nothing of whatever words of grief or passion, of remorse or indifference you may choose to send as your answer or your appeal.

His anger at the contrast between his position and Douglas' is palpable and his bitterness all too vivid. His struggle is to rise above these feelings and to see the wider view that Douglas might learn from this episode. If he is rising above – he cannot resist the swipe at Douglas:

> To you the Unseen Powers have been very good. They have permitted you to see the strange and tragic shapes of Life as one sees shadows in a crystal. The head of Medusa that turns living men to stone, you have been allowed to look at in a mirror merely. You yourself have walked free among the flowers. From me the beautiful world of colour and motion has been taken away.

This is the stuff of biography. The more enduring aspect of the text is a reflection of his views on life and art. Importantly, although affirming his previously held views on art and society, the letter acknowledges suffering – which Wilde experiences at first hand and vicariously whilst in prison, most notably in the hanging of Thomas Wooldridge who had murdered his wife – which surfaces in *The Ballad of Reading Gaol*. *De Profundis* paves the way creatively for *The Ballad of Reading Gaol*. Wilde's self-knowledge is there too:

> *I* also had my illusions. I thought life was going to be a brilliant comedy, and that you were to be one of the graceful figures in it. I found it to be a revolting and repellent tragedy ...

Subsequent to prison, Wilde was enabled by his experience to write two authoritative letters on prison reform and the treatment of children to the *Daily Chronicle*. These letters stand the test of time and must form part of any estimation of Wilde as a humanitarian. The distance between *De Profundis*, these letters and say the Preface to *Dorian Gray* could not be greater. His stories for children are the nearest in spirit.

Other parts of *De Profundis* are given over to minute accounts of the progress of the relationship with Douglas, all written in an atmosphere of reproach (Douglas has abandoned him) and attribution of blame to Douglas for his situation. This is an aspect of biography loved by those who wish to find fault with one party or another in Wilde's trials, scandal and fall from public grace. On the personal level, if it shows anything, it demonstrates how ruinously compatible they were. If Douglas dragged Wilde down, so the reverse is true. Douglas lived most of his life after Wilde's death under the shadow of the Wilde scandal. It might be supposed that this letter ended the relationship. It did not. They reunited after prison and attempted to live together. That petered out: the younger man wanted to get on with his life and have the pleasures that money could bring, whilst the older man had become needy and penurious.

The *Letters* reflect the tenor of Wilde's life from his early years to the end. They display its author in varying modes of self-expression. He could be tough, forthright as well as playful and purple. He was apt to link the serious to the local and trivial to amuse his correspondent. He debunked the 'problem of poverty', a Victorian obsession as much as our own, which avoided the obvious – that is a fairer society, by writing to Ross whilst on his visit to North Africa: 'The beggars here have profiles so the problem of poverty is easily solved.' In short, the *Letters* are both a biographer's treasure trove as well as literature, providing an insight into the age but showing too that which is not merely historical.

Journalism

Robert Ross collected the most substantial of Wilde's journalistic articles together for his 1908 *Collected Works*. As Professor Ian Small has pointed out, there is a consistency of quality of output in Wilde's work whether for a magazine or for a book. Indeed most of his prose work was published first in magazines. It was the custom of the age to publish in magazines. The Victorian reading public mostly read magazines, and these were kept in the public eye by lively articles, poems, short stories and serialisations. Books were borrowed mainly from circulating libraries and comprised mostly the three-decker (three-volume) novel. There was a constant demand for new material for magazines: this was the liveliest part of the literary market. There was money to be made by the publisher, some of which filtered down to the writer. Dickens made his fortune by journalism. Wilde would try to do the same. Why? Quite simply, he needed the money. He had a lifestyle to support and then a wife and family. What might have been more obvious – becoming an academic – was denied to him by his notoriety. He had to do what was commercially available to him. This might mean lecturing, treading the lonely boards in the United States or in some provincial town in Britain. Better to stay at home in London. He became part of Grub Street, able to turn his hand to write almost anything. He excelled, though, where others might struggle: and editors knew this. He reviewed a translation of Balzac published by Routledge:

> … Des bois de quoi se faire un cure-dent is not 'a few trees to slice into toothpicks', but 'as much timber as would make a toothpick'; …

And he concludes by saying:

> We fear Mr Routledge's edition will not do. It is well printed and nicely bound; but his translators do not understand French. It is a great pity, for *La Comédie Humaine* is one of the masterpieces of the age.

Wilde speaks with an authority which is born of profound knowledge of his subject. Neither author nor publisher can survive this sort of thing entirely intact: they can only hope that no one will read the review or take comfort in the nostrum that all publicity is good.

Wilde wrote constantly for journals as a critic. He was editor for a few years of *Woman's World*. He lost interest after a while, but in his early days as editor he tried to raise the intellectual offering by engaging established writers, including for example Guy de Maupassant, to write for the magazine. He continued to write articles through this period as well as after his editorship. This had its influence on the style, format and content of what he wrote. Robert Giddings, in his *The Author, the Book & the Reader*, charts the interaction between the modes of production, distribution and literary form. This is not so well understood in the study of literature. The author is entwined in what will pay and thus in how it is produced and sold. Books designed to be read out loud to an audience of family and friends with little else to do are different from books written in the age of cinema, television, and now instant communication. How a book is written, what style works best, becomes critical and differs from one age to another even before we take account of the fashions and foibles of each epoch.

There is an easy transition from Wilde's journalism to his published work. It may be assumed that he chose the most sustainable articles and essays to transmute into *Intentions*. With *Dorian Gray* he laboured over that transition: the book form is derivative from but differs from the magazine serialisation. Its critical mauling in the press resulted in the Preface.

Wilde was good and tough-minded enough at dealing with critical reaction in journals and newspapers: this is evident in his *Letters*. He wishes to clarify where he thinks the critical reaction was wrong. It is especially noteworthy in defence of a critical opinion he might hold, say, of Rudyard Kipling: ' ... he has seen marvellous things, through keyholes ... ', and even more so in defence of his own work – *Dorian Gray* and then *Salomé*. He knew the value of trying to get the last word. Both the letters and the critical articles repay revisiting – just to dip for the sake of pleasure and to satisfy curiosity rather than to crank the handle of a thesis.

10

Philosophy and Wit

There is a strong association between dullness and wisdom, amusement and folly, which has a very powerful influence in decision upon character, and is not overcome without considerable difficulty. The reason is, that the *outward* signs of a dull man and a wise man are the same, and so are the outward signs of a frivolous man and a witty man; and we are not to expect that the majority will be disposed to look at much more than the outward sign.

Sydney Smith, *Lectures*

IF ANYONE'S REPUTATION AS A THINKER suffered more from this judgement – other than Sydney Smith's – it is Wilde's. The notion that serious thought can be conveyed with wit is alien to the British intellectual as that term is normally understood. To such an outlook to combine wit with humour is an almost unspeakable offence against seriousness – and that is what Wilde did. Smith found that humour increased with incongruity, and that again is Wilde's method, which was joined with a genuinely Hegelian outlook on dialectical reasoning.

Why Wilde's work has survived has seemed puzzling to many critics. Serious critics have been dismissive of it (the Bloomsbury Group) or have seen it as having 'undue influence' (Martin Seymour-Smith's *Guide to Modern World Literature*). In Wilde's time some others were more discerning. Grant Allen (1844–99) a novelist, science and political writer and proponent of evolution, refers to Wilde:

> Mr Oscar Wilde, whom only fools mistook for a mere charlatan, and whom wise men know for a man of rare insight and strong common sense …

In part, continued interest in Wilde may be attributed to fascination with his biography. His name is associated with persecution of same-sex attraction and love. Biography and homosexuality are not sufficient reasons to study his work as literature – that must stand or fall as art and, in his case, philosophy.

The misunderstandings that accompany and inhibit appreciation of his work are easy enough to spot. His epigrams stand in contrast to the long mellifluous periods of his prose and verse. His work is, apart from being his means to obtain fame and wealth, the vehicle for his 'philosophy' (that is his views on what is most real, what is true, what is beauty, what is the function of art and cognate issues) which he worked upon from his Oxford days onward. It is the philosophical underpinning of his utterances, which is sometimes, but not always, apparent to the reader or the playgoer, that in a subversive, almost subliminal, sense fascinates his audience. This underpinning philosophy – sometimes expressed in the form of epigram, nearly always in the form of paradox, ensures the enduring appeal of his work.

Another issue that needs to be dealt with is the difference between philosophy and literature. Literature deals with the particular, this or that character, this or that event. It uses, in its best form, language that resonates, that suggests and makes the reader believe in what is happening whilst knowing that it is not. Plato managed in his similes such as the Cave in *The Republic* to be both an imaginative writer as well as a philosopher. Philosophy generally seeks a wider canvas, in whatever form it takes: it could be cosmological as it was in the case of A.N. Whitehead (see his *Science and the Modern World* or *Process and Reality*), or analytical as in Wittgenstein's – *Tractatus Logico-Philosophicus* or *Philosophical Investigations*, both of which examine language and its functions and limitations. Wilde philosophised, indulged in polemic advocacy via the particular. He was attracted to the idea of the parable because a parable may encapsulate an idea and make it memorable.

Even so, it seems odd in the present age to wish to combine 'wit' and 'philosophy'. Earlier ages, such as the late 17th and early 18th centuries in English literature in particular, saw such a combination as essential – along with literary style. John Locke's work for example, is a distillation of many witty conversations. Incidentally, there is much in Wilde's style of thought and assumptions that would have resonated with the 18th-century mind. He would certainly have resisted this notion as far as poetry is concerned – he, along with A.E. Housman, could not see the poetry in Alexander Pope's work. In respect of conversation, and his plays – where he sought to be 'wittier than Congreve', he concedes the affinity. Nowadays, philosophers tend to think good writing and wit to be superficial, and wits (where these exist) find philosophy dull, obscurantist or obvious. Popularisers of science and philosophy such as Richard Dawkins rarely themselves contribute insight or innovation but on the whole adopt a serious, often portentous, tone which creates, as intended, credence. Using wit to philosophise was Wilde's 'way'. Indeed the brilliance of Wilde's wit, as manifested in his aphorisms, makes his poetry and much of his prose seem by contrast, dull. But then, outside his aphorisms, he had more difficult, complex things he wished to say, as analysis of his essays shows. These difficulties repay the patience of exegesis – even if they leave a sense of frustration at their incompleteness.

Wilde had learning, an enquiring mind and a sense of

humanity which even his adoption of aestheticism with all its limitations – see the Preface to *Dorian Gray*: 'They are the elect' – did not blunt. Thomas Mann found resonances between Wilde and Nietzsche. If the Preface is taken on its own, it is all too reminiscent of Calvinism, Nazism, Stalinism and other forms of authoritarianism – burnings of people and books and self-justification. Wilde's humanity and desire to face the truth did not succumb. Contemporaries, of the more perceptive kind, believed that he had not fulfilled the promise of his evident talents. Wilde would, on occasion, admit as much himself. He had a sufficient sense of detachment to observe the human condition, and the wit and humour to communicate what he saw with a view to persuading, or at least signalling to others. His detached irony has its origins no doubt in his ambisexuality. Its essential ambiguity gave him some of his keenest insights – as we might put it – into the difference between the simplicity of our intellectual processes and utterances (the 'official' view, as it were) and the reality which, in moments of candour, we are forced to admit. 'The truth is rarely pure, and never simple.' He was against the simplifying tendency of thought – the simpler, the more elegant and true – and came closer to Wittgenstein's view in the *Tractatus Logico-Philosophicus* that not everything that we might have wished to be said, could be said.

In the individual, self-deception, and in society, hypocrisy, are Wilde's moral targets. Contradiction, or perhaps (more simply) lying and deception, are all around us – for instance – in disguising the social round of the season with etiquette whereas economic materialism and class are 'real' motives. One of the gifts of German philosophy to the 19th-century *zeitgeist* was to see how contraries produce truth: Hegel's idea of thesis – antithesis – synthesis had seeped through into British philosophical culture. Wilde had not only a keen appreciation of this, but had much fun in using it. He found in it the intellectual basis for a challenge to the orthodoxy that was so stultifying: the orthodoxy that supposed that freedom was all a man needed – not food; that marriage and property-owning was the ideal state for a person. He wanted, for his own sake, and then later to broadcast it – to discover what was true and good. He was always searching – and challenging the glib and supposedly self-evident. That he chose to do much of this in conversation, discursive essays and plays worked against him: if he were not to be taken seriously then he would make a virtue of the opposite: *The Importance of Being Earnest* is a play for 'trivial people'. Trivial people are not by definition solid followers of Matthew Arnold: they are outsiders.

The Form of Wilde's Wit

Wilde's mind was drawn to examine convention because he needed to explain his revulsion from it. More urgently, he wanted to see if the received opinion was actually true. An example would be Malthusianism in its 19th-century form

– where famine, war and disease were held to be the only antidotes to overpopulation – or indeed, as the argument became, if famine occurred then it proved that there was overpopulation. This was applied by the Victorian ruling classes to Ireland's potato famine in the 1840s (most notably) – and is described too in Booth's *Life and Labour of the People in London* where otherwise fit and healthy people died from undernourishment. What is the point of freedom (a sacred idea), he asks in 'The Soul of Man under Socialism', if you are free only to starve? Wilde's method was to turn received opinions inside out. The 'deserving poor', another popular convention, were in fact, the working poor. He debunks this by choosing the conventional 'drink is the curse of the working classes' to make it become 'work is the curse of the drinking classes'. It proposes that drinking is a more serious pastime than work, and indeed that work is a distraction from it. It debunks the trite and makes laughter. Why should the poor be grateful for charity where the system of wealth creation impoverishes the many for the benefit of the few? Significantly, this style of reasoning does not go much further, and it does not argue for moderation, Polonius-like. Indeed 'nothing succeeds like excess'. It makes the thoughtful think more, and others, occasionally, to reflect. Another, cognate form of his wit was to take the pompous at its own value: 'Alcohol, taken in sufficient quantities produces all the effects of drunkenness.' In playing with the obvious, he sought to produce delight: 'the

Book of Life begins with a man and a woman in a garden. It ends with Revelations.' As a technique it has a lasting relevance: if a politician says something ought to done, negate it and see if it makes as much sense – it usually does. What is really meant is cloaked, as much as disclosed, by language. If this is true – make an art form of it – which is what he did. What Wilde *thought*, he *applied*, in his writings, and to a significant extent, in his life.

Wilde's Strategy for Philosophy: Pursuing Ideas to their End

Wilde pursued ideas to their end: 'Nature imitates Art' for example. This was a movement of mind, if not arriving then travelling towards a general philosophical theory. He did not seem to care (or thought that it could not be done) to join up the various themes. He tried to humanise through wit that which would in other hands be pointless, cruel adherence to theory. Every age has its Plekhanovs, rigid, mechanical and inhumane ideologues of all types, whether of the 'corporate' or totalitarian state or 'the free market' upon whose ideas countless lives are wasted. The closest he came to a metaphysic that embraced politics, art and the nature of reality was in 'The Soul of Man under Socialism'.

When Wilde, disappointed in the imagination of the English he so often met, said of them that they ' … have a miraculous power of turning wine into water' (that is the reverse of Christ's miracle of turning water into wine at the wedding feast at Cana) he uttered also a truth about a style of philosophising which has characterised British and American mainstream philosophy since Hume (1711–76). In its search for what is true or most real, the empiricist school strips everything down to its minimum, supposedly irrefutable core. Thus it may not be certain that this is a table, but it is true that it is at least a patch of colour. This makes the everyday seem like an attack of migraine to one kind of sensibility – but of course it has its reasons. It is also dull.

Wilde's strategy was to turn this on its head. He used Kant's philosophy (influenced by Hume's declarations) against itself. Kant's philosophy starts with the *Critique of Pure Reason* – influenced by Hume – and analyses space, time and causation. Kant then progresses through moral philosophy – which is left no space in the world of cause and effect, culminating in the *Critique of Judgement* which explores aesthetics and taste:

> A Truth in art is that whose contradictory is also true. And just as it is only in art-criticism, and through it, that we can apprehend the Platonic theory of ideas, so it is only in art-criticism, and through it, that we can realise Hegel's system of contraries. The truths of metaphysics are the truths of masks. ('The Truth of Masks')

Wilde, using a neo-Kantian view of perception, reversed this convention, starting instead with the aesthetic feeling, which in turn revolves around perception. What do we see?

And what relation has this to the real? These age-old questions, and a variety of answers philosophers give, were familiar to Wilde. Whilst he knew Plato's theory of forms, he did not see our perceptions as if they were shadows of the real, dancing on the walls of Plato's cave. He was closer to Aristotle's perceived reality which comprised matter and form conjoined. This was his earthiness, usually (but not wholly) dismissive of any 'occult' type of reality. He could see the sense also of perceptions and the categories of mind, space, time, causation, combining to create 'our' reality. He took this argument further in 'The Critic as Artist', that Art influenced or created this perceptual process; thus Nature imitates Art. Were there really London fogs before Whistler painted them, he asks? We might say perhaps only those fogs that Dickens wrought in his prose. How we see things is vitally important – a victory in battle for one side is merely a re-grouping for the other side. A Goebbels-style reality, the everyday product of the media, is with us. The only antidote is perceptive wit. This came naturally enough to Wilde – nurtured by growing up in a family of intellectuals. But he also laboured over honing that wit: it was all to prove a point.

Enjoyment of the senses is the starting point – and Art has the role in stimulating these senses and thus creating the 'reality' which we experience. This is the rationale for his assertion that London's fogs did not exist before Whistler painted them. Whatever we may say, post Whistler we do view London fogs rather specially. If the expression of doubt is the engine of modern philosophy, who can doubt the feelings say of pleasure or revulsion on experiencing something? Taste in all its aspects plays a large part in creating the world we inhabit. The invitation to view reality philosophically in a different way is intriguing. But where does it lead?

Art and taste, and the role of art criticism have their functions in society, and in particular forms of society that allow art to flourish. For Wilde, this is modelled by the ancient Greek *polis* or city community which self-governs and is prosperous enough to sustain artistic endeavours and where enough people have the ability to appreciate and criticise art. This is one of the germinal ideas to be found in his university essay 'The Rise of Historical Criticism' published many years after his death. Aristotle's oft-quoted dictum that man is a political animal is based on a somewhat misleading translation. Wilde and later H.D.F. Kitto correct this by saying that man is understood to be part of this cultural *polis* or city state. It cannot be asserted too strongly that classical Greek culture, language and philosophy ('Hellenism') were important to Wilde. It is fundamental to understanding how his views developed.

In 'The Soul of Man under Socialism' he refers to the possibility of an emergent society as the 'new Hellenism' where the vital ideas of classical Greek culture could be realised in the modern age. He theorised that in the coming era machines would do the menial back-breaking work relieving the toil of people which in ancient Greece were undertaken by slaves, so that the circumstances would emerge where people would be free to be themselves. As Aristotle says, and Wilde quotes in his *Oxford Notebooks*: ' ... if the hammer and the shuttle could move themselves, slavery would be unnecessary ... ' The centrality of Aesthetics to Wilde's thought cannot be overemphasised – it was not an affectation – it was a passion and a starting point, as his *Oxford Notebooks* make clear:

> **Beauty**
> Art is one though the service of art is diverse. Beauty also may become incarnate in a myriad of divers forms but the worship of beauty is simple and absolute. [185] (Commonplace Book)

Dandyism: Dress and Mentality

Wilde was a Dandy: he took more than pride in his appearance – his carefully posed photographs were designed for a specific effect. In order to be, he had to dress the part. As he developed his thinking, new influences would be announced in his dress. As the prophet of Aestheticism or Art for Art's sake – he wore his hair long and wore breeches and velvet jackets. Reading the works of Balzac in Paris, he wore the monkish habit of Balzac. Under the influence of Baudelaire he cut his hair short and wore sober clothes. The importance of dress for women ('Woman's

Dress', 1884) as well as for men was a preoccupation of his. The staging of plays depended on dress (see his essay: 'The Truth of Masks').

When in 'Pen, Pencil and Poison' Wilde wrote on Wainewright, poisoner, forger, poet, artist, he referred to Wainewright's Dandyish instincts:

> Like Disraeli, he determined to startle the town as a dandy, and his beautiful rings, his antique cameo breast-pin, and his pale lemon-coloured kid gloves, were well known and indeed were regarded by Hazlitt as being the signs of a new manner in literature ...
>
> ... This young dandy sought to be somebody, rather than to do something. He recognised that Life itself is an art ...

Wilde could have been (and surely was) writing about himself.

On Being Yourself

It is presumed that *knowing* yourself is the precursor to being *yourself*. But how do we come to know ourselves? It is a process of discovery through the events of life. The idea of temptation intrigued Wilde. For him, feeling tempted by something is a clue to who you are. A temptation had to be pursued: 'I can resist anything except temptation.' In this fundamental way, he challenged the idea of self as being accessed solely via contemplation. A pupil of Pater and then a companion, he lived Pater's advice to live for the moment and to pursue it relentlessly – ' … tear the heart out of it … ,' he would say – which the more timid Pater found alarming. It was a burden too: he admitted once that he hardly knew who he was. He reached the point reached by Kierkegaard: the aesthetic man is driven hither and thither by his passions, contrasted with the autonomous man. Being pushed around as it were was not Wilde's view. *The Picture of Dorian Gray* is amongst other things a sustained thought-experiment to see where the doctrines of hedonism and aestheticism lead.

Concept of the Soul

The injunction to know yourself and then to be it suggests that there is a fixity about the soul, self or mind. 'Be yourself,' Wilde says, 'everyone else is already taken.'

Ryle's *The Concept of Mind* (1945) created controversy by suggesting that the idea of the mind (or soul) as a ghostly presence that operated on the human body was wrong. He used the phrase 'ghost in the machine' to express that view. Wilde's view of the mind was similar to Ryle's:

> There can be no knowledge of human nature without knowledge of the Laws of Mind, (Psychology) nor of the Laws of Mind without knowledge of the Laws of Life (Biology). [7] (Commonplace Book)

Wilde was, after all, a doctor's son. He believed in the unity of body and soul.

Ryle's ideas were resisted as soon as they were published. Such ideas usually are – but there is an inherent absurdity in dualism which is shown by this extract from Andrew Marvell's poem, 'A Dialogue between the Soul and the Body':

Soul
O who shall, from this dungeon, raise
A soul, enslaved so many ways?
With bolts of bones ...
... here blinded with an eye ...
A soul hung up, as 'twere, in chains
Of nerves, and arteries and veins, ...
In a vain head, and double heart.

Body
O who shall me deliver whole,
From bonds of this tyrannic soul ...

This excerpt shows, in a way that reams of philosophical argument do not, the difficulties of the idea of the ghost in the machine. Ryle had an unacknowledged debt to Aristotle. Wilde embraced and acknowledged the influence of Greek thought and was as close to the Greek ideas of the soul – one version of which would be Plato's tri-partite division of the soul – broadly, the intellect, the virtues (moral restraint and guidance) and the passions or senses.

Wilde tested this out also. 'To cure the soul by means of the senses and the senses by means of the soul' is more than a rhetorical flourish. The intellect, then, is conditioned by the passions and the passions restrained by the virtues.

Free Will and Determinism

Wilde's greatest difficulties, in common with most people, related to the notion of the self, or the soul as it used to be called. He did not subscribe to Hume's notion of the soul as being a mere bundle of sensations. He did believe that there was soul, a perceiving, thinking, feeling being. This 'soul' or self has an essential nature, which, if it is to be fulfilled, or be a '*eudaimon*' (Greek) or crudely, to be a fulfilled (happy) person, has to discover and then express or follow that nature. 'A patriot put in prison for loving his country, loves his country,' he once remarked. Over the portals of the Ancient World, he declared was the inscription 'Know Thyself' – the Oracle at Delphi – whilst over the portals of the modern world is 'Be Thyself'. In this, he is close to Spinoza. In the sense that the test is both to know and then to be, he is close to Schopenhauer, who saw the 'will' as the ultimate reality. At his harshest Wilde allows no claims on the 'personality'. He quotes Christ in saying 'Let the dead bury the dead.' But, then, sentimentally and superstitiously, he was a fatalist. He consulted palm readers (see 'Lord Arthur Savile's Crime'), and for himself could see no escape from a pre-ordained fate.

Love and Humanity

Wilde's fatalism in his work, but not necessarily in his life, was saved by his ideas of love and the need to 'humanise' actions – that is, consider the effects on others of actions taken and things said. Dorian Gray might be physically beautiful, but his soul is not, caring only for hunted animals, but prepared to ruin the lives of fellow human beings. Love is the conquering tone in his plays, with the need for reconciliation, acceptance, compassion and forgiveness. Its interpretive force is implied by *The Importance of Being Earnest*. The *crime passionnel* of *The Ballad of Reading Gaol* shows that love negated makes a man somehow happier to face death than to endure continuing to live.

Love and Passion

Wilde sought to understand sexual passion, desire, possession and love. It could not be both felt and readily denied if a full life is to be led. He marvelled at how the object of desire could also override a life in a set course, or principles held to hitherto, and produce unforeseeable and disastrous consequences. Salomé's passion for John the Baptist is a case in point. But even in passion Wilde still sought love. His plays point to it, in particular *An Ideal Husband* and *The Importance of Being Earnest*, but his post-prison letters state it clearly.

Love is a mysterious, all-enveloping force, 'Poor wounded

fellow … ' he wrote of Ernest Dowson on hearing of his death ' … for he knew what love *is* … ', and in the exchanges of love, misunderstandings and otherwise inexplicable actions occur. Dowson, too, was Wildean: he could not understand why his love for a girl should 'so upset his spiritual economy … ' but it did. Dowson pined for this girl, but compensated for this, or rather tried to, by a resort to prostitutes. Wilde's passion for Bosie was as ill-starred and compensated for in a similar fashion. The paradoxical nature of human relations was pointed to, and illuminated by Wilde: he saw them also as unavoidable. Solecisms of style – see some of the prose poems – are ameliorated to an extent because the mission is philosophical and polemical.

'The Soul of Man under Socialism':
Politics, Society and Freedom

Wilde sought to integrate his ideas – where he thought he had succeeded in his views on Art and perception, the self and love, and wanted then to put them into a social and political analysis. What Wilde learned from the reception of *Dorian Gray* was that direct description created difficulties. Same-sex love would be rejected as unwholesome – 'morbid' – 'morals of a telegraph boy'. But these difficulties could be the emblem of the difficulties of all love and passion, regardless of the object of passion. His integration of these apparently contradictory states – same- and opposite-sex love – was a minor dialectical victory. It also proved to be a formula, in writing plays, for commercial success. His best synthesis is in *Earnest*. Freedom of expression – one of the most friable of freedoms – is an aspect of the freedom to be what you are.

The relationship of such libertarianism to society as a whole is always problematic. Much as Wilde delighted in the sensuality described in *Dorian Gray*, other issues such as poverty, starvation and oppression concerned him. The clearest expression of this concern is in 'The Soul of Man under Socialism', probably written after hearing a lecture by Bernard Shaw on Socialism/Marxism. This prolonged speculative essay delineates a picture of a possible coming age when machines do the tedious work, freeing people to become cultured, autonomous beings. Art would have a central role in society: he called it the 'new Hellenism'. The machine age would be a socialistic age, relieving people of the onerous responsibility for property. The landed classes would always complain about the responsibilities of property ownership: Wilde says – opt then for a society without property ownership. Genuine socialism would obviate the need for charity – which he sees as odious – expecting thanks for giving back that which was appropriated in the first place. Wilde's views were not those of economics, the science of scarcity, but rather of the science of plenty (copionics). There is plenty – share it about. Relieved of the need for property, the marriage contract itself would be different and people would marry for love. If this is a Utopian vision, so be it: we need Utopias. He saw, presciently, the possibility of authoritarian socialism (ochlogarchy – the tyranny of the majority) which would negate the value of socialism since it would be more oppressive than the existing system. He admitted that he was treading the difficult line of what we might now call left-wing libertarianism. In line with his essential Darwinism (see *Dorian Gray*) he also subscribed to the idea of progress, influenced by Herbert Spencer's ideas about social evolution.

It is possible that Wilde's positions cannot be made into a coherent philosophy: Isaiah Berlin in the 20th century thought that freedom and equality are not commensurable. This means in effect that at some point we have to choose one or the other. Wilde's incommensurables are freedom and responsibility for the means of life; freedom of the individual and social responsibility; realisation of the individual through art, ecstasy and living in society.

Jesus and Parables

Wilde loved to use the form of the parable – short oral stories, some of which he committed to paper – to illustrate his point of view. He copied what he saw as Jesus' way of enlightening his audience. He was obsessed with Christ, but not in the conventional way. He could see that through parables Christ could provoke and shape thought. Christ's parables resonate down the centuries because they are stories. We are all brought up on stories. We like them because they have beginnings, middles and ends. They have an ability to suggest the truth as well as to deceive: 'and they lived happily ever after'. He saw Christ as a man rather than as a divine figure. His view of the meaning of Christ's words is opposed to conventional Church-led readings. Wilde saw Christ as a revolutionary in the sense that he saw the main issue was how to live free and unencumbered: 'Let the dead bury the dead.' In 'The Soul of Man under Socialism' and later in *De Profundis* he dwells on his view of Christ. In *De Profundis* this becomes an obsessional over-identification with Christ. Wilde really did want to change fundamentally our concept of ourselves, and with that, of society. Looking into a figure of authority, which Christ is, and using Christ's mode of expression, the parable, was a way of doing this. He was in conflict with established authority taking on the Church and Christianity as the 19th century saw it: especially with the views of Protestants. He could not see, for example, that the granting of further life to a man who habitually sinned would lead to anything more or less than a continuation of sinning. The notion of Redemption is under scrutiny. He was a Darwinist in the sense that he could believe in the causality argument for evolution – he was not a political Darwinist (neither was Darwin) who seemed to hold that the survival of the fittest entailed the neglect of his fellow human beings.

He sought to escape the strictures of Protestantism by

joining the Roman Catholic confession. In his young days
– he signally backed away, only agreeing to enter the Church
as he received the last rites as he lay dying. He needed love
and forgiveness.

Forming a true estimate of the philosophical value of
Wilde's thought is not easy. If a fully thought out position,
with discussions of arguments and counter-arguments is
sought, it is not there. His thought is polemical; it advocates
a position. It darts here and there, covering a wide field. It does
not rank with, say, Schopenhauer. But, like Schopenhauer's
work, it is provocative and readable. And if to challenge
orthodoxy – to see if it is true and to propose other ways of
thinking – is philosophy, then Wilde's work, in the way that
prose may be described as poetical, is described more
accurately as philosophical.

Wilde and Parables

Flaubert's *The Temptation of St Anthony*, inspired Wilde. It
showed the use of the religious experience and parable to
convey quite other messages. Religious ecstasy for one
person is a set of material phenomena for another
(Flaubert's 'A Simple Heart' – *Trois Contes*). Wilde adopted
this form eagerly. This dual aspect is what he needed to
express himself. On the brink of conversion to Rome, this
Protestant, Anglo-Irish Freemason pulls back and sends
flowers to the expectant priest. Having to choose one path
is to denude the man, and more especially the artist, of his

essential being. Reality is a larger thing figuratively, than black or white – it is both. Wilde becomes a preacher – see *De Profundis* for his most direct statement on this. His conversation, when in full flood was to tell a 'story'. He would use an existing form and change it for his purposes. He was seemingly better in full flood at the dinner table than at his desk. Read his prose poems and then compare his story of 'The Early Church' recorded in Richard Ellmann's biography of Wilde to see this point. In speech, he was unaffected and direct, using the medium of the voice, its modulations, gesture and presence to substitute for the elaborate prose that is sometimes a 'dud' on the page. The essence of *Salomé, La Sainte Courtisane* (the holy whore), is to go into the conventional tale to see what is really there – as in the case of the more directly sexual – it is complex and of mixed motives. The holy, the biblical, Egyptian, Arabic, were all ways of exploring candidly what human beings are, without opprobrium (not us! them! and not now, but all those years ago!). Looking into the past is altogether superficially 'safer' but no less provocative.

The fruit of Wilde's speculations is to be found just as much in his stories and plays as in his essays. The prose poems and short stories are abbreviated forms of his findings – and his paradoxes, aphorisms are, as it were, the condensate.

In looking at Wilde's 'philosophy' what emerges? It makes sense to see it as if it were a map:

The structure of reality is one of change, uncertainty and apparent contradiction;

Metaphysical constants are the soul or mind or indeed the community of minds;

The mind is an active principle – not merely passive in receiving perceptions – it shapes them – and the way it shapes perceptions changes as the mind itself develops as it would through education and the experience (in the high street sense of the term) of living. The highest form of apprehension in art is the sense of the beautiful and the pleasure taken in the contemplation of it;

Living – what you may live for, what you do is *the* activity – this is what it is all about. Living is enriched by art and the exchanges entailed – the critic as well as the artist. Criticism is a creative act. Art acts not only on the intellect but on the perceptions and the perception of beauty is the most enriching;

You will live best if you understand your own make-up as a person. Understanding what that make-up is, is one duty; acting upon that understanding is the other;

Living socially is about love and compassion – not charity in the sense of giving to the poor, but making sure that there are no poor people. It is holistic in the sense that to wish for freedom, let's say from slavery, is incomplete unless you make provision for freed people to be able to eat and sustain themselves. Much nowadays is made of people being freed from cruel and undemocratic rulers – only to find countries plunged into civil war, brutality and starvation;

Technological advance should make possible a new way of life that uses the opportunity of leisure to create a cultured, perceptive and full life for everyone. This is the Utopia worth striving for – unburdened of property on the one hand and starvation on the other, there is a possibility of a better life, where relations amongst people are not contaminated by these burdens;

More than all of these, maintain a critical view bearing in mind these principles especially concerning the nature of reality and the nature of mind. Wit reveals through contrasts, not only what there is but what could be.

The biggest constraint on his philosophising was the mode of expression he used – the poem, the novel, essays, plays – whatever was commercially available to him. He needed an income. He had no significant independent income or academic salary. He earned his living by his pen. Necessarily, then, his work is fragmentary and incomplete. It is suggestive of something bigger rather than expressing it fully. Polemical, it selected what should be addressed, what could be overlooked. His reasoning merits our attention. In his *Oxford Notebooks* he declares:

Philosophy passes into mysticism because it cannot answer its own questions: the highest truth of philosophy is rational and self-conscious poetry: and the highest poetry is often irrational and unconscious philosophy. (183. Commonplace Book)

11

Wilde's Legacy: Atoms of Genius

WILDE HAD A 'PROJECT', AMBITIOUS, SWEEPING and aimed at the universal. He wanted no less than to change the ways in which we all think. His first position, which is now more often accepted than it once was, but almost as often forgotten, is to challenge the received 'wisdom' whatever it may be. It is not pleasing to those people in authority who want their way with things whether at the political level or in endeavours of the intellect, the dreaded 'peer group'. He wanted the rigours of both science and philosophy, and he knew about both. More than that, he knew how to use ideas and push at the boundaries of thought. To quote again from *The Picture of Dorian Gray*:

'The way of paradoxes is the way of truth. To test Reality we must see it on the tight rope. When the verities become acrobats, we can judge them ... '

Accordingly, the method was to oppose the commonplace – 'the verities' and to see where the thought process might lead.

As to the project itself, it may be inferred that it was humanistic and materialistic. Pagan thought and feeling for nature relieved what might otherwise become an arid, stifling and mechanistic outlook. His view of aesthetics reinforced this position. As a result of these ideas, he found a place for both passions that are recognisable and the intellect in human life and knowledge. He enlists the figure of Christ in making his point of view, but not in a way that conventional Christianity would recognise. He uses the *story* or the *parable* as did Christ as a way of communicating and challenging ideas.

We make the world we inhabit, Wilde says, so why not make it a pleasanter place? Aesthetics represents the pinnacle of human experience: art actually *makes* the world as we know it. It would be better for all if we acknowledged it. Commercialism and economic materialism of all kinds afflict our lives. He thought that if we take property out of relationships it would transform marriage, for a start. He thought we would be better served by living in city states rather than mass society with the tyranny of ownership.

From his student days he saw the *polis* – the city state of Greek society – as ideal. In the modern era people would be able through the device of machines (rather than slaves as ancient Greeks had) to lead more leisured lives with the possibility of realising the ideal of the contemplative life. He called this the 'new Hellenism'.

In our age, we have accepted the idea of *challenge* as if it were almost a commonplace. He proposed *a way* of making that challenge. His ideas were tested out in conversation, poems, prose and plays. He needed the feedback that an audience provided to move his thinking on. In his last years he was deprived of this necessary stimulus. He was exhausted, in declining health and unable to see much beyond the financial exigencies of each week. In Paris, he once begged from a famous actress some money saying 'Pour finir ma semaine'. The result is an array of fragments of the great project: 'those atoms of genius' scattered about. The project was unfinished. The full frontal attack on received opinion apparently, had not succeeded. But it has not entirely failed, either.

The nature of Wilde's wit bears examination: it is why he amuses audiences today and remains quotable. He is able to represent the complex in simple ways – to hint at much more without stating it. He is able to suggest another point of view opposed to the conventional one. This power of suggestion comes from a philosophical outlook that commenced in his university days. This philosophical outlook derives from his ideas about metaphysics, aesthetics and moral and political philosophy.

The nature of reality rests on human perception where he fuses ideas about beauty and art as representing the ultimate or founding nature of the world. His ideas about morality view moral truths as being founded on self-realisation, not on abstract principles. In this sense he would seem to be similar in outlook to Spinoza, but in Wilde's case it is founded on a trust in nature that is essentially pagan. His ideas about politics are no less than to change economics and society. It is necessary to do away with the nature of property and its insidious claims on people's lives. The inequality that is endemic in property and ownership of capital make it outrageous that the poor should be grateful for 'alms' when the system works to deprive them of the means of existence. He mentions specifically the marriage contract which is property-based and distorts relations between men and women. He sees the opportunity represented by technology where machines undertake repetitive work, to make possible the creation of a society of people devoted to the creative, contemplative life. Society itself would be best organised along the lines of the *polis* or the Greek city state. The synthesis that is happening here is between the classical Greek philosophical outlook as represented by Aristotle and of course Plato and modern technology.

In literature in the English-speaking world for a long

time his contribution was seen as marginal, the creation of a 'buccaneer' and interloper. His theories were disdained. The Bloomsbury group described him as 'cabotin' (poseur). Their opinion of themselves was ludicrously high, just as their opinion of everyone else was disdainful. There has been a revival of interest in Wilde, driven in part by the rise of the campaign for equal rights for people whose sexual orientation is other than the conventional, heterosexual. *The Picture of Dorian Gray* and 'The Portrait of Mr. W.H.' are iconic texts. The hand of support from this camp of people has helped ensure aspects of Wilde's legacy. A.E. Housman's poem 'Oh Who is that Young Sinner' written – but not published – at the time of Wilde's trials and imprisonment is indicative of this:

> Oh who is that young sinner with the handcuffs on his
> wrists?
> And what has he been after that they groan and shake their
> fists?
> And wherefore is he wearing such a conscience-stricken
> air?
> Oh they're taking him to prison for the colour of his hair.
>
> 'Tis a shame to human nature, such a head of hair as his;
> In the good old time 'twas hanging for the colour that it is …

The Picture of Dorian Gray continues to be read. Wilde's poetry is collected and published in new editions. His plays are regularly revived as classics of the theatre. His ability to command attention through his work has waxed rather than waned. The biography industry has thrived on Wilde's life story. More interestingly, fragments of his work and letters surface from time to time. People want to know what he has to say.

In literature in English, more directly, writers such as H.H. Munro ('Saki') defended Wilde's reputation as a scholar and writer and wrote witty stories along Wildean lines. Kenneth Grahame in his *The Wind in the Willows* uses Wilde as the model for Toad whose extravagant career lands him in prison 'for insulting a policeman'. He shows that the creatures of the Wild Wood that invade Toad Hall will be expelled and that Toad will be restored to his rightful position. Ronald Firbank followed in Wilde's footsteps in writing first in the decadent style *Odette d'Antrevernes* and then picking up the lightness of touch and conversational mode of 'Lord Arthur Savile's Crime' to develop his own style of writing in *Inclinations, The Flower Beneath the Foot* and *Concerning the Eccentricities of Cardinal Pirelli*. The last is surpassingly ironic, satirical and amusing. Evelyn Waugh and then later the playwright Joe Orton used language in a similar way to Wilde. These writers tended to be the men in mauve, so to speak: all same-sex sympathisers to a greater or lesser extent. Just as these people followed and supported

Wilde, the opposition to Wilde rested on hostility to some extent at least to Wilde's sexuality.

In philosophy, continental Europe with its attachment to bigger ideas has found Wilde more interesting than did the English-speaking world. Parallels between Wilde, Schopenhauer and Nietzsche have been observed. *Salomé* stands higher there than here, for example. Gide in his literary-philosophical way found inspiration in Wilde's ideas, and for a long time he had a seminal influence.

In the English-speaking philosophical world in recent decades a revision of opinion of Wilde's work has been under way. Gilbert Ryle admired Wilde's style of writing and thought. *The Concept of Mind* is a long debunking of mind-body dualism which shows how unnecessary it is. Both Ryle and Wilde shared a common heritage of admiration and learning in Greek philosophy and literature.

However, one of the best examples of this revisionism is Julia Prewitt Brown's book *Cosmopolitan Criticism: Oscar Wilde's Philosophy of Art*, which gives a serious, and by the far the best, treatment of Wilde's aesthetics.

In continental Europe, Wilde's reputation was made initially in the odium caused by the Boer War (1899-1902) – a particular type of British imperialistic cruelty and inhumanity. Wilde died in 1900, and as another victim of the British Empire, automatically found favour. Critical estimates of his work started on a higher plane. He was described always as a poet in France and Germany. For many years in Britain and Ireland this was seen as the least estimable aspect of his work. *Salomé* was seen from the start as significant – a critical view led by Maeterlinck himself as the leader of the Symbolist movement. Wilde's impact in France tended to grow with the passing of time: Pierre Louÿs may have rejected Wilde, but Louÿs remained a writer dedicated to sensuality. Louÿs's friend André Gide was for a time overwhelmed by Wilde. Wilde appears in *Les Nourritures Terrestres* ('Fruits of the Earth') as the character Ménalque. Wilde's philosophical outlook is represented there. In modified ways Gide carried ideas based on it forward in his own work.

Wilde's work is subversive in the sense of providing a platform for criticising conventional, received wisdom. The style of his wit, which uses the devices of paradoxes and contrasts to make a point, still works. It began in his lifetime. The influence it has is best illustrated by the following cameos. The first is taken from Richard Ellmann's biography of Wilde. Wilde was standing accompanied by a prison warder, on a railway station away from Reading where he had been jailed to avoid the attention of the press and public, just prior to his release from prison. Travelling *incognito* as it were, Wilde seeing a magnolia bush in bloom exclaimed, with his arms wide open: 'The world, the beautiful world!' to which the warder riposted: 'Come now, sir, there is only one man in England that talks like that, on

a *railway station.*' And as reported by Stanley Weintraub in
Reggie, whilst Wilde lay dying he said melodramatically to
his friend Reggie Turner: 'Last night I dreamt that I had
died and was supping with the dead', to which Turner
replied: 'I am sure that you were the life and soul of the
party.' Who could fail to respond to such an Essence?

Bibliography

Principal books consulted

Works

There are many versions of Wilde's works dating from Robert Ross' *Collected Works* published in the early 1900s. The 1912 edition of *Salomé* introduced by Robert Ross is quoted in this book. Ross did as much as he could to keep Wilde's work in the public eye. This collection has been largely superseded by:

Complete Works of Oscar Wilde, published by Harper Collins, (1994).This is ideal for the general reader. It contains the four-act version of *The Importance of Being Earnest*. Whilst this is of interest, the three-act version the author edited and issued in the late 1890s should also be read – and be regarded as definitive for that reason: see below.

Oscar Wilde, The Importance of Being Earnest and Other Plays, edited by Peter Raby, Oxford English Drama (2008). This has the three-act version of *The Importance of Being Earnest*.

The Picture of Dorian Gray, edited by Robert Mighall, Penguin Classics (2000). This is a scholarly, well-annotated and edited edition. Indispensable.

Oscar Wilde's Oxford Notebooks; A Portrait of Mind in the Making, edited by Philip E. Smith II and Michael S. Helfand, Oxford University Press (1989). Many notes are made to Wilde's original comments. These *Notebooks* help explicitly to establish Wilde's status as a thinker. If confirmation were needed of internal evidence of Wilde's work, this is it.

Letters:
The Letters of Oscar Wilde, edited by Rupert Hart-Davis, London (1962); this is an invaluable service to students of Wilde's work. It provides information on the key figures with whom Wilde corresponded and provides an insight into the age: indispensable.

More Letters of Oscar Wilde, edited by Rupert Hart-Davis, published by John Murray, London (1985)

Biographies

There are many, many biographies of Wilde. Some seem rather pointless eg by St John Ervine, seemingly motivated by malice, some rather one-sided, eg Philippe Jullian, dismissive of Wilde's marriage, etc. I indicate below those I found most informative and balanced:

Oscar Wilde; A Critical Study by Arthur Ransome. Methuen (1912): this biography is perceptive and sympathetic. Douglas caused difficulties over its publication. Its literary judgements as well as the account of Wilde's life withstand scrutiny.

The Life of Oscar Wilde by Hesketh Pearson. Penguin (1946 and 1954): this is a very interesting and useful book and did much to restore Wilde's reputation as a writer and a man. The author spoke to people who met and knew Wilde, and so must be regarded as of value on these grounds alone. It is a sympathetic work: some regard it as bordering on the hagiographic.

Oscar Wilde by James Laver, Writers and their Work. Longmans and the British Council (1956): one of the best, concise overviews of Wilde's life and work, by a scholarly author.

The Paradox of Oscar Wilde by George Woodcock. Boardman (1950), possibly intended as a companion to Hesketh Pearson's biography – gives a critical estimate of Wilde's background and work. Woodcock was an anarchist writer and tends to emphasise that aspect of Wilde's thinking.

Oscar Wilde by Richard Ellmann. Penguin (1988): the definitive biography. It covers Wilde's life as comprehensively as possible and is a fair-minded commentary also on his life and work.

Oscar Wilde: The Importance of Being Irish by Davis Coakley. TownHouse, Dublin (1994): this provides an essential insight into the Wilde household, the influence on Wilde of Irish cultural figures, the politics and ethos of the time. Wilde retained his belief in political autonomy for Ireland. The contemptible approach of the British government to Ireland led Wilde to make clear his own nationalistic views in his reviews and in his works.

Constance: The Tragic and Scandalous Life of Mrs Oscar Wilde by Franny Moyle. John Murray (2011): this is an incisive account that provides a different and vivid perspective on this impressive woman, the Wildes' complex relationship as well as Wilde's own nature.

Son of Oscar Wilde by Vyvyan Holland. E.P. Dutton & Co. (1954): written by Wilde's second son (Cyril was killed in the First World War). This makes clear the impact of Wilde's scandal on his wife and family. Humanly, this is essential reading.

Mother of Oscar: The Life of Jane Francesca Wilde by Joy Melville. John Murray (1994). Background reading – but shows how important she was both to Oscar and to the cultural history of 19th-century Ireland.

Adam International Review – a literary monthly in English and French edited by Miron Grindea, nos. 241, 242, 243 (1954) – centenary of Wilde's birth: comments from leading literary figures from Britain and France, including people who knew Wilde.

Critical Essays and Other Background Reading

Cosmopolitan Criticism: Oscar Wilde's Philosophy of Art by Julia Prewitt Brown. University Press of Virginia, Charlottesville and London (1997 and 1999). This book treats Wilde's aesthetics with due and proper attention. This work deserves to be well known.

The Eighteen Nineties: A Review of Art and Ideas at the Close of the Nineteenth Century by Holbrook Jackson. Grant Richards, London (1913). It sheds light on this remarkable decade and gives a critical estimate of Wilde's work – but whilst acknowledging the 'Everyman' aspect to Wilde, proposes his limitation as his sexuality.

The Aesthetic Adventure by William Gaunt. Cardinal, London (1975). This is a lively, readable account of the revolt against the most tedious and grinding aspects of Victorian commercialism and industrialism. Ruskin, Pater, Morris, the Pre-Raphaelite Brotherhood, Whistler, Wilde are placed in the context of the times.

Essays and Biographies by A. J. A. Symons. Cassell, London (1969).This book has three perceptive essays on Wilde. These are the remnants of a projected but never completed biography of Wilde.

Oscar Wilde: A Collection of Critical Essays, edited by Richard Ellmann. Prentice-Hall, New Jersey (1969). This collection indicates the evolution of critical opinion on Wilde, including excerpts from Pater, André Gide, W.B. Yeats, Borges, Joyce, Auden and others, and poems by Johnson, Douglas, Brendan Behan.

Complete Poems of Lionel Johnson, edited by Iain Fletcher. Unicorn Press, London (1953). The introduction by Iain Fletcher is, if not definitive, impressive.

An Anthology of 'Nineties' Verse, edited by A.J.A. Symons. Elkin Mathews & Marrot (1928). Symons was a talented writer of considerable perception and taste, and along with Desmond Flower kept the spirit of the Nineties alive

Poets of the 90's by Derek Stanford. John Baker. London (1965). Stanford, ever the champion of the 1890s, brought the poets and their poetry to the attention of 1960s audiences.

Poetry of the 1890s, edited by R.K.R. Thornton. Penguin (1970). Professor Thornton is an authority on 1890s poetry and together with Professor Ian Small has kept 1890s poetry in print.

Decadent Poetry from Wilde to Naidu, edited by Lisa Rodensky. Penguin (2006). This is an interesting collection with concise and useful notes.

The Renaissance by Walter Pater. Macmillan (1889). This is a seminal work in aesthetics of the late nineteenth century.

Appreciations by Walter Pater. Macmillan (1893).

The Aesthetes: A Sourcebook, edited by Ian Small. Routledge & Kegan Paul (1979).

Six Sonnets by John Barlas, edited and introduced by Iain Fletcher. Eric and Joan Stevens (1981). Iain Fletcher did more than anyone to recognise and to promote the merits of 1890s poets. His introduction to Lionel Johnson's *Poems* has not been surpassed.

Collected Poems by Lord Alfred Douglas. Martin Secker, London (1919).

The Poetical Works of Ernest Dowson, edited by Desmond Flower. Cassell (1967).

Ernest Dowson: Poetry and Love in the 1890s by Henry Maas. Greenwich Exchange (2009). A well-informed and intelligent account of this lyric poet.

The Letters of Ernest Dowson, edited by Desmond Flower and Henry Maas. Cassell (1967). Dowson and Wilde were on friendly terms, both in 'exile' in France in the late Nineties.

Letters of Aubrey Beardsley, edited by Henry Maas, J.L. Duncan and W.G. Good. Cassell (1971). Beardsley illustrated *Salomé*. Wilde did much to promote Beardsley.

Reggie: A Portrait of Reginald Turner by Stanley Weintraub. George Braziller, New York (1965). The biography of Reggie Turner, a close friend of Wilde, who attended Wilde in his last days.

Beardsley by Stanley Weintraub. Pelican Biography (1972). Beardsley illustrated Wilde's *Salomé* – Wilde did not admire the illustrations.

Ronald Firbank: A Biography by Miriam J. Benkovitz. Weidenfeld and Nicolson (1970). This biography shows how Wilde's work and reputation exercised a hold over succeeding writers.

The Rise of the Russian Empire, by H.H. Munro. Grant Richards (1900). This is a piece of audacious (and amusing) history and demonstrates, in passing, a sympathy for Wilde's persecution. Munro's (Saki's) work shows Wildean influences in terms of style – but not in terms of philosophy and political thought. Munro was conservative by nature.

From Dickens to Hardy: The Pelican Guide to English Literature, edited by Boris Ford. Penguin (1964 edition). Wilde is positioned in his epoch.

A Shropshire Lad and *Collected Poems* by A.E. Housman.

A.E. Housman: Spoken and Unspoken Love by Henry Maas. Greenwich Exchange (2012) refers to Wilde in the poem 'O Who is that Young Sinner?'. This is a concise, balanced and sympathetic account of Housman and his work.

Against Nature (À Rebours) by J.K. Huysmans, translated by Robert Baldick. Penguin (1966). This is a seminal text which had an enormous influence on Wilde's thought.

Three Tales (Trois Contes) by Gustave Flaubert, translated by Robert Baldick. Penguin (1965). See 'Herodias', which inspired *Salomé.*

Engaged by W.S. Gilbert, available on line. Possibly this play is the inspiration behind *The Importance of Being Earnest.*

The Quest for Proust by André Maurois, translated by Gerard Hopkins. Pelican (1962). Maurois' account of Proust is penetrating, lively and accessible. The issue of same-sex relations is freely discussed and is present in Proust's *Remembrance of Things Past (À la Recherche du Temps Perdu)*, translated by C.K. Scott Moncrieff. Moncrieff did much to introduce Proust to the English-speaking public, referencing Shakespeare in the title rather than the more accurate 'In Search of Lost Time' used by subsequent translators.

André Gide, *The Journals 1889–1949*, edited and translated by Justin O'Brien. Penguin (1967). Gide was overawed by meeting Wilde – Gide was a friend of Pierre Louÿs who assisted Wilde with *Salomé*. Wilde's influence was direct in terms of Gide's philosophical outlook. See especially Gide's *Fruits of the Earth*.

Pierre Louÿs (1870-1925): A Biography by H.P. Clive. Clarendon Press (1978). Louÿs was a friend of both Wilde and Gide and broke with both of them. He was a writer whose career spanned the 1890s but no further, whose interaction with Wilde produced interesting insights into both men.

Collected Poems and Other Verse by Stéphane Mallarmé, translated by E.H. and A.M. Blackmore. Introduction by Elizabeth McCombie, which gives an invaluable insight into the French literary scene, where Wilde is seen as an admirer and friend of Mallarmé. Oxford University Press (2008).

Lives of the English Poets by Samuel Johnson. Everyman's Library (1964). See essay on John Dryden.

The Smith of Smiths: Being the Life, Wit and Humour of Sydney Smith by Hesketh Pearson. Hamish Hamilton (1934). The Reverend Sydney Smith was like Wilde, in that he was a great conversationalist, wit and observer of human nature, with a sharp eye for hypocrisy.

The Greeks by H.D.F. Kitto. Penguin (1991). Background reading on classical Greek society.

Nicomachean Ethics by Aristotle, translated by W.D. Ross. Oxford University Press (1966).

The Republic by Plato, translated by A.D. Lindsay. Everyman (1964).

INDEX